Get Set Mum

THE COMPLETE GUIDE
TO BUYING FOR BABY

©2020 Get Set Ready
Self-published by Angela Miller

GetSetMum.com

 GetSetMum @GetSetMum

Design by ©2020 **stowlo.co.uk**
Images from ©AdobeStock and Unsplash

ISBN 978-1-913717-12-4

THE COMPLETE GUIDE TO BUYING FOR BABY

Angela Miller

Hello.

There are certain events we all experience that
are thoroughly life-changing, and becoming a parent
is certainly one of them. It is one of the most exciting
adventures you can embark on – but it is equally
terrifying, particularly when you're a first-timer.
With the average baby costing £10,000 in its first year
of life you wouldn't be alone if you're thinking
'How much do I need to buy?' and 'How much
will my baby cost?'

Get Set came to pass in 2018 following two major life events I experienced in quick succession. First, in June 2018, we were blessed with the birth of our first child, Miles, and then, just three months later, I was struck with the sudden loss of my mother. As I embarked on this incredible but equally overwhelming roller coaster journey of first-time parenthood, another unexpected journey began.

As I was planning the funeral it reminded me of when I was pregnant and how surprised I was that there wasn't one simple resource that focused on the practical components of preparing for this major life event. During pregnancy you have to make so many decisions in a short space of time with an accompanying never-ending 'to-do list'. I wanted something that would guide me each step of the way, from what to do week by week (such as medical appointments, work admin and antenatal classes) to knowing what to buy for baby (and why), and how to prepare for labour. And so, I spent hours searching the internet, talking to friends and picking up advice here and there, but failed to discover one destination for quick and easy resources that helped us get organised and make decisions with confidence.

Coming from a career in international business development, where planning and preparation are paramount to success, I naturally wanted to apply these skills to help bring about positive change around some of the issues I personally faced, and to support individuals going through the same experiences.

Launching with *Get Set Mum*, our mission is to bring you content and planning tools from experts and parents alike, who know what you are going through so you can successfully navigate your pregnancy journey with confidence and ease. *Get Set* every step of the way!

Angela Miller
AUTHOR

First of all, congratulations to you, our expectant parent. The countdown is now on until 'birth-day!' We know for all expectant parents, welcoming a (teeny-tiny) member of the family into your lives is life-changing!

So where do you start?

During your 42 weeks of pregnancy,
you'll find yourselves needing to make
a myriad of decisions in order to prepare
yourselves and your home for baby's arrival.
You will also find there is no shortage of
information and opinion out there to
overload and confuse you.

Firstly, don't panic! Secondly, remember
this is an exciting time with joyous
new experiences, learning for you and
for baby, and a totally new phase of life
for the whole family.

Our Complete Guide to Buying for Baby brings you:

 Snap Explainers

Demystify all the categories of baby-buys as you prepare your home for the new arrival. Position yourself to make quick decisions on:

- ▶ **What you need to buy and what you don't**
- ▶ **Why, how and when parents use each item**
- ▶ **Side-by-side product comparisons**
- ▶ **Budget allocation and priority**

 Minefield Simplifiers

We cut through the complexity around some of the most important baby-prep items and provide a 360° view that's balanced and backed up by experts. Topics are presented in a digestible manner and allow you to make confident decisions about what's best for you and your baby including:

- ▶ **Baby safety**
- ▶ **The nappy debate**
- ▶ **Car seats and which types to opt for**

 Get Set Tools

Your toolkit of easy-to-use checklists and templates, readily available to download and personalise so that you can:

- ▶ **Easily track your progress**
- ▶ **Review products side by side**
- ▶ **Remember what to pack and never leave home having forgot an item**

As we guide you through the items for your baby-prep, there are a few that would be considered essential for when baby comes home. The rest are nice-to-haves or non-essential investments that you can decide on post-baby; either because you do not need the item until later on or you decide it will be beneficial to you and baby.

Whether you choose to purchase the non-essential items before baby comes or after will depend on available budget, space at home and personal preference.

Throughout the book you can recognise **Essential Items** by the full circle symbol ● and **Non-essential Items** by the half circle symbol ◗

Contents

☀ SNAP EXPLAINERS

LITTLE ONE'S ROOM 11

OUT & ABOUT 23

BABYWEAR 33

FEEDING TIME 41

SPLASHTIME & CHANGING............................ 55

PLAY & DEVELOP 63

HEALTH & SAFETY 69

MUMMY MATTERS 77

⠿ MINEFIELD SIMPLIFIERS

SIDS 84

THE NAPPY DEBATE 88

CAR SEAT INTEL 104

≈ GET SET TOOLS

HOSPITAL BAG: WHAT TO PACK 116

NAPPY BAG MUST-HAVES 120

THE ULTIMATE CHECKLIST 122

PRAM PICKING MADE SIMPLE........................ 126

CAR SEAT SELECTOR 130

SNAP
EXPLAINERS

The Complete Guide to Buying for Baby

01

LITTLE ONE'S ROOM

> A MOTHER'S JOY BEGINS WHEN NEW LIFE IS STIRRING INSIDE;
> WHEN A TINY HEARTBEAT IS HEARD FOR THE FIRST TIME AND A PLAYFUL KICK
> REMINDS HER THAT SHE IS NEVER ALONE.
>
> **Anon**

SLEEPING

Many parents like to get the nursery set up
before baby's arrival, but it is not essential and there
are several items you can purchase at a later stage.
In fact, current guidelines recommend parents
should keep their baby in the same room as them
for the first 6 months – not only to help promote
parent-baby bonding, but research has shown
it can help protect your baby from Sudden Infant
Death Syndrome (SIDS).

Learn more about SIDS on page 84.

We've provided a list of the 'sleep stations' you can
choose for your baby. These are not all essential
– you just need to select one, ready for when baby
comes home. Anything else is a personal choice,
for example, if you want a secondary sleep
station or a portable option.

⬤ Moses Basket & Mattress

The traditional moses basket is still an old favourite and a great choice. One benefit is that it's portable and lightweight, which makes it easier for you to move baby around the house. There are hypo-allergenic versions available that are easy to wipe down and sterilise (versus the wicker style).

The moses basket is more compact than a bedside crib but you might find that your baby will outgrow it at around 3–5 months (depending on size). As such, you could use it as a secondary sleep station for naps, however, some parents will opt to have this as baby's primary sleep station.

Bedside Crib & Mattress

A bedside crib fits nicely next to the parental bed and will often come with legs adjustable to different heights (suitable for various bed designs). It will have a removable or foldable side, allowing you to easily move baby into your arms and bed for those night-time feeds or when you want to quickly reach over to soothe them.

One helpful feature of this type of crib is that you can elevate/lower the legs at one end, which is useful for common issues such as reflux and colds (helping your child to breathe easier through a stuffy nose/chesty cough). Do refer to the manufacturer's guidelines as this will advise the maximum level of elevation for that crib – it will also detail the maximum weight limit, so bear this in mind for when your baby is a little older and getting ready to be moved into their cot or bedroom.

Sleeping Pod/Nest

These are essentially mini mattresses with padded sides that offer a snug sleeping area for your baby. They are becoming increasingly popular as an alternative to the traditional moses basket as they provide a lightweight and portable sleeping space.

Pods come in two sizes and the current age guidance is:

▶ **Birth to 8 months**
▶ **9–36 months**

If you have a baby born on the higher percentile you may find they will outgrow their pod much sooner than the brand advertises. Although a popular product and endorsed by many parents, an important consideration is that these are not recommended by the *UK Department of Health* in conjunction with *The Lullaby Trust* because of the soft mattress and cushioned area.

Cot & Mattress

There are many cots available that will grow with your child. For example, there are different height settings; the highest setting suitable for when your baby is first transferred into their cot and the lowest for when they get bigger (toddler stage). There are models available that convert from cot to bed (this is where the sides can be removed from the main frame) and so provide longevity and better value for money.

When you purchase a cot you will also need to consider which mattress you will buy. The mattress should be:

▶ **Firm**
▶ **Waterproof**
▶ **Entirely flat** with no soft cushioned areas, particularly around the baby's neck

Public Health England guidelines recommend checking that the sleeping item conforms with British Standards, which it should say on the product, packaging, instructions or website. This means it has passed certain tests, including not falling apart or easily setting on fire.

GET SET *tip*

TO AVOID CHANGING YOUR
MATTRESS SHEETS FREQUENTLY
FROM A 'SICKY' BABY, FOLD A
MUSLIN CLOTH AND LAY IT OVER
THE MATTRESS SHEET (BABY'S
HEAD END) AND TUCK IT IN
TIGHTLY UNDER THE MATTRESS.
THAT WAY, YOU ONLY NEED TO
REPLACE THE MUSLIN RATHER
THAN THE SHEET.

Mattress Sheets

Sheets will be required for each sleeping
station and we would recommend two of
each, just in case there are any accidents,
so you can put a fresh one on while washing
the other.

Waterproof Mattress Cover

Some mattresses come with a waterproof
cover attached, but if not, you should
purchase one for every sleep station
(cot, bedside crib, moses basket). You
can buy either:

▶ **A lay flat waterproof sheet**
▶ **An elasticated cover** that folds under
  the mattress

Changing Mat

A changing mat is a cheaper alternative to
the changing table. These are foam-based
mats covered in a PVC lining, which is easy
to clean and portable. If you live in a multi-
storey house you may want to buy two mats
– one to leave upstairs and one for downstairs.

Blankets

It is always useful to have a mixture of blankets
of different thicknesses that you can use at
home or on-the-go. Consider the season
you are giving birth in along with room
temperatures to ensure you use a suitable one.

If you are using a blanket to cover baby when
sleeping, make sure that it is not too thick
to prevent overheating, is tucked in tightly,
and comes no higher than their shoulders (to
prevent the blanket from moving over baby's
head when wriggling).

Baby Monitor

Audio & visual options are available with some useful features to soothe baby like music, projecting light patterns or animals, and a 'talk back' function that allows your baby to hear your voice without you having to enter the room.

Some brands offer a 'Movement Sensor Pad' that sits under the mattress your baby sleeps on or a clip that attaches to your baby's nappy. Both the pad and clip will offer similar assurances as they are designed to monitor your baby's breathing and movement. Should there be no movement for a given period of time, the monitor will alert you and the clip will make a sound so you can immediately check on your baby.

Baby monitors are also good to take with you when travelling, although there are baby monitor mobile apps available for these purposes as well.

Baby Monitor Holder

It can be a struggle to find the perfect spot to place the baby monitor especially if you do not have a flat surface nearby to rest it on. A holder will give you more flexibility and options on where to place the monitor within the nursery – it can even attach to the cot, which will provide you with a better view of your (hopefully) sleeping baby.

Room Thermometer

Rooms across your house can vary in temperature. As such, you may want a baby thermometer dedicated to the room they sleep in to avoid them getting too hot or too cold. UK guidance suggests the ideal room temperature is between 16–20°C.

Most room thermometers will have a colour system easily showing you if the room is too hot (red), cold (blue) or just right (yellow). If the room feels too hot or too cold to you, remove or add layers of your baby's clothing and/or adjust the room temperature accordingly.

CONSIDERATION:

Many baby monitors have an integrated digital temperature reader so a separate room thermometer may not be a necessary purchase. And with the likes of Google Nest and Hive you can always keep the little one's room temperature just right.

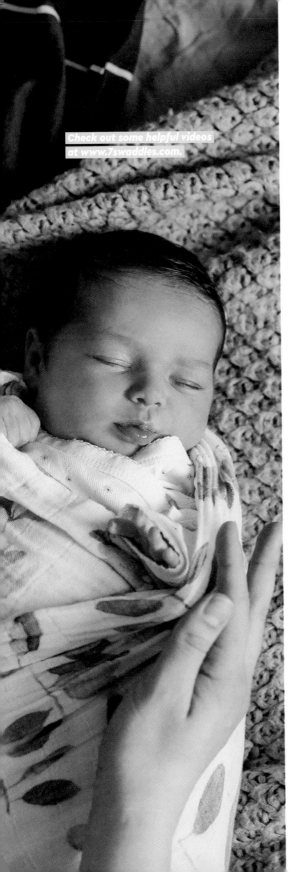

Check out some helpful videos at www.7swaddles.com.

Swaddles

'Swaddling' is a style of wrapping that helps imitate the compactness and comfort of being in the womb whilst keeping baby cosy and secure. There are different swaddling techniques and recommendations based on a baby's age. As you and your baby establish a routine, you will quickly ascertain whether this option works for you both.

There are a few different types of swaddles available including:

▶ **Velcro™ Wrap** – Traditional wrap used in conjunction with a swaddle blanket/cotton cloth that secures the material and baby with a Velcro™ fastening.

▶ **Zipped Wrap** – Comes with a zip opening to place baby in with two sides that you wrap over baby for a snug fit.

▶ **Zipped Swaddle/Sleepsuit** – Comes with a zip opening and, rather than a wrap to secure baby's arms, they are placed in enclosed sleeves. This style is a more modern version.

▶ **Cotton Cloth (i.e. a larger muslin)** – Can be used in hand with a Velcro™ wrap or on its own (depending on room temperature). There are plenty of designs and colours to make swaddling fun and the larger cotton cloth can be multi-functional:

- To place baby on the floor for playtime
- An additional layer for warmth
- A winding cloth
- A breastfeeding cover

17

Wardrobe

This is not an essential item if you have room in your wardrobe for baby's clothes, but it's certainly something to consider for the nursery and for when you need the extra space.

Chest of Drawers

You may find a chest of drawers is more beneficial than a wardrobe as it can provide additional storage space to organise your baby's clothes, muslins, blankets, sleeping bags, nappies, creams etc.

Changing Table

Many of the options available are multi-functional compared to the changing mat. You will want to consider the types of tables there are, how much space you have, personal preference and budget before deciding if you need this item. Options include:

▶ **Cot Top Table Changer** – A changing table that sits on top of the main cot (not the bedside crib) and is great where space is limited. Can be easily attached and removed.
▶ **Standing Station Changing Table** – They will often come with shelves and open compartments for extra storage and easy access to nappy changing items. These are kinder on parents' backs!
▶ **Integrated/Dresser Changing Unit** – Often doubled up with a chest of drawers, this looks aesthetically pleasing as a piece of furniture. The changing facility sits atop with multiple drawers offering plenty of space for nappy changing items and clothing underneath. Like the standing station, this will put less strain on parents' backs.

Nursing Chair/Rocking Chair

Some parents love these as they offer a comfortable option for feeding and quality time with baby, not to mention the calming rocking motion for both baby and parent! This type of item will very much depend on space available, personal choice, and budget.

Lambskin Comforter

Natural lambskin provides insulation and ventilation, keeping little ones warm in the winter and cool in summer, as well as a soft place for baby to lay on. It can also act as a liner for your carrycot, keeping baby nice and snuggly – some are adapted specifically for pushchairs (as they come with holes to thread the harness/straps through to secure baby).

Lambskin wool is considered hypoallergenic, so it should not aggravate or cause a reaction to baby's sensitive skin.

As a general rule, if using lambskin for bedding you should cover it with a sheet and place baby on their back. Once baby is ready to roll over you need to remove the lambskin until they can move about easily and hold their head up (approx. 12 months). Always check the manufacturer's guidance.

Blackout Blinds/Curtains

These blinds are ideal when you want to block out sunlight on long summer evenings and early dawns. It can support your child getting to sleep easier/having a better sleep.

You can purchase blackout blinds or curtains to fit the exact window measurements in the room your child is sleeping in or, alternatively, purchase portable blackout blinds, which will fit most window shapes; the length and width can be adjusted using the sewn-in poppers/Velcro™ and attached using suction pads.

GET SET *tip*

SEARCH FOR WHITE NOISE APPS ON YOUR PHONE AND PLAY THEM AT HOME OR WHEN OUT AND ABOUT TO SOOTHE AND CALM YOUR BABY.

White Noise Machine

White noise is a sound that reduces background noise and provides a consistent and soothing backdrop to aid a better night's sleep (should your child have trouble sleeping). There are different types of white noise sounds including nature sounds (jungle, rain, waves, crickets chirping) and ambient sounds (crackling fire).

CONSIDERATIONS IF YOU CHOOSE THIS DEVICE:

▶ **One gadget, multiple features** – A number of night lights or toys come with built-in white noise sounds, therefore you could purchase one item for multi-purpose use.

▶ **Noise level** – Always ensure the noise level is not too high and is placed at a safe distance to prevent long-term hearing damage.

▶ **Dependency** – Your baby may not settle without this to go to sleep.

▶ **It may not work** – Your baby may not respond to white noise. Like many things when first having a baby, this will be trial and error.

Always read the manufacturer's guidelines for specific product usage.

Cot/Crib Bumpers

The Lullaby Trust does not consider bumpers safe because of accidents that can occur once your baby starts rolling and moving. Some parents still like the option of these as they provide protection against the hard cot bars. Therefore, look for bumpers that offer breathable material and come with Velcro™ rather than ties; if you use ties, you should ensure they are secured tightly to help reduce the risk of baby becoming caught.

Cot Mobile

Mobiles act as a sensory toy for your baby to engage with as they stare up at the ceiling looking at the colours and patterns. The music played from the mobile can be soothing although slightly limited, therefore you can always play your own music via another device, for example, a phone, home sound system, bluetooth speaker.

Projector Night Light

A night light can provide ambient mood lighting with shapes, animals or colours gently washing across the ceiling. Each baby is different, so you'll just need to ascertain that it does not act as a stimulus or distraction to them going off to sleep. Alternatively, use it as part of a sensory activity during the day.

Bookshelves

Placing bookshelves on walls helps to organise all those lovely stories you will read to your baby, not to mention it will free up floor space that will quickly become occupied with all your other baby bits.

Framed Pictures

Decorate the nursery with family pictures, prints of animals or other images based on the theme of the nursery to create an atmosphere of warmth, love and positivity.

Wall Art

If you have a theme for your nursery you can paint a design (should you be so creatively gifted) or use any number of themed stickers, which are easy to apply to the wall. Stickers can be removed at a later date (by applying heat on a warm setting from the likes of a hairdryer).

Spiral Cot Toy

This is a simple and great toy for the cot and pram that provides stimulation and entertainment through colours, sounds and soft hanging toys. It encourages motor development when baby reaches, pulls and squeezes it.

02

OUT & ABOUT

BEING A MOTHER IS LEARNING ABOUT STRENGTHS YOU DIDN'T KNOW YOU HAD...
AND DEALING WITH FEARS YOU DIDN'T KNOW EXISTED.
Linda Wooten

PRAM: CARRYCOT AND PUSHCHAIR

This is one of the most expensive items you will purchase, so you want to make sure it meets your needs and requirements. Pram systems are typically sold as a set (including a carrycot and pushchair) and have longevity since they will carry your baby from birth until they can walk freely.

● Pushchair

Once baby outgrows the carrycot you can move your baby into the pushchair, which can be used until they reach a maximum weight of approximately 22–25kg. Again, each brand will have their own guidance, but to give you a clearer idea, this weight is typically anywhere from age 4 and up. So it's safe to say you will get good value for money using the pram system. Pushchairs will often have a:

▶ **Rearward-facing mode** – Where baby faces the person pushing, giving them comfort of sight and allowing the person pushing to engage with baby.

▶ **Forward-facing mode** – Is where the baby faces the direction of travel and is typically used once their development shifts, meaning they've become more alert to their surroundings and eager to see what's going on around them (head and body movement is a good signal of this).

If you are having twins or want a second child within 3 years, consider:

▶ **Dual seat system** – A pram that converts in this way will give you the option of configuring your pram as follows:

- Carrycot + carrycot
- Car seat + pushchair
- Pushchair + pushchair

▶ **Vertical configuration** – Some prams that accommodate two are configured horizontally, which makes mobility on pavements and manoeuvring around obstacles somewhat challenging, therefore you may prefer vertical configuration.

● Carrycot

You will start with this, which your baby lies flat in for the first 6 months or until they start sitting up unaided/reach an approximate weight of 9kg (each brand may have small variations on the maximum weight allowance so just check the manufacturer's guidelines). The lie-flat position is particularly important to support proper spine and hip development and optimal breathing.

GET SET *tip*

SHOULD YOU PURCHASE THE LIE-FLAT CAR SEAT YOU WILL NOT NEED A CARRYCOT. THIS KIND OF SEAT DOUBLES UP AS BOTH A CAR SEAT AND CARRYCOT (AND IS SUITABLE UP TO 9KG). JUST CHECK YOU CAN SECURE THIS SEAT TO THE PRAM FRAME AND THEN PURCHASE THE PUSHCHAIR ONLY.

PRAMS CAN BE VERY BULKY, SO BEFORE MAKING YOUR FINAL PURCHASE TEST THAT IT FITS WELL INTO THE BOOT OF YOUR CAR.

Travel System

This simply means being able to remove the car seat from your vehicle and securing it safely onto the frame of the pram (using adaptors). Check that the pram adaptors are compatible with your car seat of choice or that you can buy separate adaptors that will work. Otherwise, purchase your car seat as part of a bundle from the pram supplier as many have this option (car seat, carrycot and pushchair).

Accessories

▶ **Rain cover** - Attaches to the top of the pram frame covering the pushchair/carrycot and should be supplied with the pram. If for any reason the brand you opt for does not provide one, we would recommend you buy it separately.

▶ **Large-sized shopping basket** – All prams come with some storage, but size varies so check this when browsing.

▶ **Pram organiser** – Is a handy holdall solution that can attach to the handlebar of your pram, allowing you quick and easy access to items such as house keys, mobile phone, dummy, wet wipes and maybe even treats! An ideal solution when you're on the go with baby and don't want to rummage around the nappy bag or pram basket.

▶ **Cup holder** – Pushing your child is thirsty work, so rather than digging into your rucksack or pram basket, a cup holder is secured to the pram frame and provides easy access to your beverage of choice, and keeps you hands-free whilst you stroll.

GET SET *tip*

YOU CAN PURCHASE SEPARATE BUGGY CLIPS THAT ATTACH TO THE HANDLE OF THE PRAM ALLOWING THE NAPPY BAG (OR YOUR SHOPPING) TO BE CARRIED. THESE ARE WIDELY AVAILABLE AND PROVIDE ADDITIONAL SUPPORT FOR WHEN ON THE MOVE WITH MULTIPLE BAGS.

Go to page 126 – 'Pram Picking Made Simple' for a fill-in template that will help you research, compare and decide on your ideal pram.

● Car Seat

Knowing what car seat to buy is one of the more tricky and expensive purchases as parents learn about safety standards and what's important to them in a car seat and why as they wade through all the products out there. Our Minefield Simplifier will break this all down to help make the decision and buying process a little smoother for you.

Go page 104 to read our 'Car Seat Intel'.

Go to page 130 for your 'Car Seat Selector' Get Set tool.

● Baby-on-board Sign

If you have a car, get yourself one of these signs as it will alert drivers that you have a baby in the vehicle as well as emergency services in the event of an accident.

GET SET *tip*

PACKING YOUR NAPPY BAG THE NIGHT BEFORE CAN HELP YOU FEEL LESS RUSHED ON THE DAY OF YOUR OUTING AND IS A USEFUL HABIT TO GET INTO.

● Nappy Bag/Rucksack

The nappy bag can be a rucksack or holdall, although you'll tend to find rucksacks comfier for everyday use; they free up your hands and ease the pressure on your back. The benefits of a nappy bag include:

▸ **Specifically-designed compartments** to hold those essential items such as bottles, milk, nappies, wet wipes, toys and baby clothes

▸ **Travel changing mat**

▸ **Matching pouch** often purchased separately, useful for holding items like cream, socks and medicine

▸ **Fun and stylish options** to suit your style and taste (at varying price points)

Never leave home without something you need. Go to page 121 for your 'Nappy Bag Must-haves' checklist of what to pack each time you go out.

● Weekend/Travel Bag

When travelling you will need a slightly larger bag for multiples of everything. Some brands offer a weekend/travel bag as an additional accessory to the rucksack, which is great if you would like matching items. Equally, you can just use your own weekend/holiday suitcase and put your baby's clothes in with yours.

Stroller/Buggy

Strollers or buggies, as they are often called, are a lighter and more compact version of a pushchair. If you wanted one of these you wouldn't need it until your baby is sitting upright unaided and has strong neck muscles (although some brands do offer suitable versions from birth). Many parents like this as an option for out and about when baby is older for the following reasons:

- ▶ **Lighter**
- ▶ **Easily foldable**
- ▶ **Space efficient** – Takes up less space in the car boot, when stored indoors or walking on pavements
- ▶ **More mobile** – Easier to move from one mode of transport to the other and in crowded places
- ▶ **Functional** – Gives little feet a respite from walking or to comfortably have a daytime nap

Pram Liner/Footmuff

These provide warmth and cushioning for your baby when being pushed in the pram during those colder months, with holes positioned so the harness and crotch straps can be threaded through. They come in different fabrics but you should look for one that provides optimal temperature regulation and moisture control to prevent your child from overheating.

The main difference between the two is that the footmuff comes with a detachable zipped exterior cover, which is often water-resistant, meaning baby can be kept fully protected from the elements, or it can be removed and used solely as a liner. The liner can be used all year round for general comfort especially if you use a breathable fabric, which keeps babies cool in the summer and warm in the winter, e.g. lambskin wool.

Rearward-facing Mirror

Your baby can be rearward-facing in the car for anywhere up to 4 years of age, and so these mirrors have been designed to fasten easily onto the centre of a rear seat headrest, allowing the driver to glance in their rear-view mirror and check on baby.

Car Window Shades

A cover that attaches to the car window to help protect baby from the sun's harmful UV rays, reduce the sun's glare and minimise heat. These are ideal during the sunnier months and will help shield your baby's eyes from the sunlight. Even where cars come equipped with tinted windows, the additional shade might be beneficial.

Sleeping Pod/Nest

as detailed in our 'Little One's Room' chapter, a sleeping pod is:

- ▶ **Lightweight** compared to a travel cot although not as compact for transportation
- ▶ **Portable**
- ▶ **Easy to transport** with the accompanying travel bag – you may have to purchase this separately

Travel Cot

A travel cot is a portable bed used for baby when travelling, and:

- **Easily opens and collapses**
- **Is accompanied with a travel bag** making it compact and easy to carry in 'transportation' mode
- **Permitted on board most flights** as free additional luggage – just drop it off at the oversized luggage counter once you have checked in
- **Generally cheaper** than a sleeping pod
- **Offers longevity** since they are suitable from birth to 3 years or 15kg. Refer to the manufacturer's guidelines for exact details
- **May come with an attachable bassinet** for newborns that's inserted inside the cot, which means it's also suitable as a sleep station at home.

If you have a moses basket or carrycot (suitable for sleeping in overnight) then this provides an alternative to a travel cot in baby's earlier months. Some parents will opt for a pod instead of a travel cot, however, *The Lullaby Trust* does not recommend these in their safe sleeping guide due to the soft mattress and cushioned areas.

Nappy Pouch

A pouch is useful when you are out and about and do not want to carry your whole bag for a quick nappy change. It can hold a small number of nappies, sacks, wipes and creams. If you buy a nappy bag and this does not come with a pouch, then you can purchase this as a separate accessory.

Baby Carrier/Sling

A baby carrier/sling is an alternative method for carrying your child and is often a harness/cloth that is secured around the carer's back and chest. This is a completely hands-free option while supporting baby and allowing you to go on those long walks without a pram or vehicle. This closeness also promotes the baby bond and aids their development.

A sling that is comfortable for one parent might be different for the other and you both want to feel good going out exploring with your baby, therefore it's worth taking some time to test out the different products on the market.

Finding the right baby carrier/sling

BABY SLING LIBRARY
Look for one in your nearby area where representatives demo the different styles, carry positions and brands of slings – allowing you to 'try before you buy'.

PRIVATE 1-1 SESSIONS
These might be useful if your budget allows; a typical session can cost approximately £30 per hour. Both parents can take their time trying on different slings and testing comfort with baby (if you go after baby's arrival).

HIRE
As an alternative to buying, some companies provide a 'hire' service. This only works out cheaper if you are hiring for a short period of time (around £30 for 2 weeks vs £250 for a year).

Sun Parasol/Shade – for pram or stroller

It is important to keep your baby cool when out and about. Parasols are like mini umbrellas that clip onto your pram /pushchair providing shade to protect your little one's sensitive skin from the sun's harmful rays. Should you have a pram hood that is deep and provides fuller coverage that you are satisfied with, you may decide you do not need a sun parasol. But if you do, look for a parasol with:

▶ **UV-protected Lining** (at least SPF 50+)
▶ **Flexible arm/base** – To help you easily move the parasol into place, providing the appropriate shading for your baby
▶ **Pram compatibility** – Not all sun parasols are universal, i.e. will fit every pram. Most brands will offer a parasol as an additional accessory to purchase for your pram system

Sunshades come in various styles offering partial coverage of the pram/stroller to full coverage. Those that offer full are useful when on-the-go and your baby needs sleep, not just providing shade but blocking out most light. They come with a zip for quick access to check on baby and for additional air circulation, although the material should also be breathable. Refrain from using items that prevent the air circulating like muslins, blankets and cloths.

For more information on 'Baby Summer Safety' visit www.lullabytrust.org.uk/ safer-sleep-advice/baby-summer-safety/

Sun Parasol – for beach or park

When you take a day trip and are in an open space such as a park or beach with little to no shade, it is advisable that you have a sun parasol that provides protection for your baby. Many parasols offer a UV protective lining and should be at least SPF 50+.

Formula Powder Pots

Formula pots are small and portable so before you leave the house, you can spoon in the exact quantity of powder needed per bottle feed – then when you are out, simply pour the powder into your bottle (with boiling water and wait for it to cool to the desired temperature), ready for when baby needs a feed.

Travel Bottle & Food Warmer (Thermos Flask)

This is a portable and compact thermos flask that you can take anywhere with you to add water to powdered formula or to warm up milk and baby food. It should be small enough to pack in your nappy bag.

Dummy Steriliser

If your baby loves a dummy then you may want a dummy steriliser at the ready. When a dummy falls on the ground you simply place it in the steriliser (with a backup already inside ready to be swapped out), leave it there for the time advised (around 15 minutes) and it's ready to be used again. The steriliser is an alternative solution to having antibacterial wipes and is quickly accessible since you can attach it to the frame of your pram. Should you not use a steriliser, put a couple of backup dummies in your nappy bag/pouch – you would be surprised how easily misplaced they are.

GET SET *tip*

ANOTHER USE FOR THE LANYARD IS TO TIE A PRAM TOY TO IT (NO DUMMY) AND CLIP IT TO YOUR BABY'S CLOTHING OR PRAM. WHEN BUBBA THROWS IT, WHICH THEY WILL, THE TOY WILL NOT HIT THE FLOOR AND THEREFORE WILL NOT REQUIRE CLEANING.

Lanyards

These are used to attach a dummy onto your baby's clothing and help prevent the dummy falling out of your baby's mouth onto the ground.

Travel Steriliser – for feeding equipment

Many mothers like to start off breastfeeding, so it is worth waiting to see how you get on before deciding if you need a travel steriliser. Whether you offer formula/ expressed breast milk from the outset or move to this feeding method, you will need something to sterilise the bottles while travelling. A few options include:

- ▶ **Steam steriliser** – A plastic container that can hold multiple bottles and is placed in the microwave. Often cannot hold larger-sized bottles
- ▶ **Specially-designed milk bottles** – Can be sterilised independently in a microwave thanks to a silicone insert inside the bottle that you add water to
- ▶ **Cold water steriliser** – A plastic bucket is filled with water and a steriliser tablet added before placing the bottles inside – ideal for plane travel or long car journeys
- ▶ **Saucepan** – Place bottles upside down in a saucepan of water and bring to the boil

Travel Play Mat

Having a play mat that's light, easily foldable and washable that you can pop in a bag or car when seeing friends and family is very handy, particularly if you are spending a night or more away. It acts as a play area for your baby whilst adding extra cushioning to the floor.

03

BABYWEAR

THERE'S NO WAY TO BE A PERFECT MOTHER AND A MILLION WAYS
TO BE A GOOD ONE.
Jill Churchill

Baby clothes come in an array of sizes but just like buying for yourself, the size and fit can vary depending on the material and brand. Add in the fact that babies are constantly growing and it can be confusing knowing what sizes to buy.

In the first two years baby clothing will cover small age ranges, for example, 0-3 months and 3-6 months, to accommodate the speed at which a baby will grow. All babies are unique and their sizes will vary, so it's perfectly normal to keep your baby in one size for longer before moving them into the next age range, or move them up earlier.

To provide some form of reference, we have put together an indicative sizing chart based on our research of UK retailers and the weight/height their baby clothing typically fits:

AGE (MONTHS)	PREM/EARLY	NEWBORN	0-3	3-6	6-9	9-12	12-18	18-24	24-36
Weight (lbs)	Less than 7	7-10	10-13	13-17	17-19	19-22	22-24	24-27	27-32
Height (cm)	Less than 50	50-56	56-62	62-69	69-74	74-80	80-86	86-92	92-98

GET SET *tip*

SHOULD, OR RATHER WHEN YOU
ENCOUNTER A NAPPY EXPLOSION, DO
NOT FRET ABOUT TRYING TO TAKE THE
BODYSUIT OFF OVER THE BABY'S HEAD.
BODYSUITS HAVE BEEN DESIGNED IN
SUCH A WAY THAT ALLOWS YOU TO PULL
THE MATERIAL DOWN STARTING AT THE
SHOULDERS, TAKING BABY'S ARMS OUT
AND PULLING IT DOWN THEIR TORSO
AND OFF FROM THE FEET.

Bodysuit

This is a cotton layer that you can dress your
baby in, which covers their torso and arms
(their legs will not be covered in this type
of suit). They typically have three poppers
at the bottom (nappy section) to secure it
and come in varying sleeve lengths:

▶ **Sleeveless/vest style**
▶ **Short-sleeved**
▶ **Long-sleeved**

It is advisable to purchase a mixture of
these bodysuits, as they are ideal for layering
under other items of clothing like a sleepsuit
or outfit to add extra warmth. In addition,
take into consideration the season your baby
will be born in to ensure you are prepared
with the relevant layers.

You can purchase bodysuits individually,
in sets or within multi-packs, and often
in a variety of patterns and colours. These
are the clothes that will likely be worn,
stained and replaced the most. So, if you
have an expensive one, be warned!

Sleepsuit or Baby Grow

These two names can often confuse parents
due to different retailers using both names
to advertise what are ultimately the same
product! Sleepsuits and baby grows are
cotton-based outfits with long arms and
long legs to keep baby warm and snug.
Some brands that typically originate from
hotter climates will offer short-sleeved
options too.

There are variations to the sleepsuit, which
can include:

▶ **Built-in feet covers** (to keep little
feet warm)
▶ **Open feet**
▶ **Built-in hand mittens** (to prevent
scratching)

Zipped sleepsuits are becoming more popular
and offer a quick and easy solution for getting
your baby in and out with minimal disturbance
to them; a game changer compared to the
more traditional buttoned/popper sleepsuits.

GET SET *tip*

A GOOD RULE OF THUMB
IS TO DRESS YOUR BABY
IN ONE MORE LAYER THAN
YOU ARE WEARING FOR
THEM TO BE COMFORTABLE
IN THE SAME ENVIRONMENT.

Romper

Like sleepsuits but without feet and mittens, the romper can be used for sleeping or for an occasion, as some are quite dressy. It might be nice to have an alternative style to the standard sleepsuit as it is fairly typical for babies to spend their first 6 months in these types of outfits (unless there's a special occasion to dress up for).

Jackets/Cardigans

It is always good to have additional layers for your baby depending on the season and occasion. If you have a good knitter in your family or friend network, then expect one or two!

Beanie/Woolly Hat

Your baby will come into this world having been in a warm and cosy environment. As a baby loses a great deal of heat from their head it is advisable to place a hat on their head to help keep them warm and regulate their temperature. This is particularly important when they're first born, leaving the hospital or in a cold environment.

Sun Hat

A sun hat is essential for protecting your baby's head from direct sunlight and should be considered if your baby will be born during the summer months. When leaving the hospital, you can use the sun hat in place of a woolly hat. Beanie hats can be quite thin and a suitable alternative.

Outfits

The number of outfits your baby will have depends on various factors such as whether you have a girl or boy, your preference on how you like to dress your baby and what gifts you receive!

As your baby will grow at quite a pace in their first year we suggest buying outfits for different age brackets, so you're prepared for when they suddenly need to move into the next size (0–3, 3–6, 6–12 months, etc). If friends and family want to buy baby clothing it is always a good idea to ask for bigger sizes since you will most likely be well stocked up with the smaller ones (both from your purchases and gifts). And remember, there is plenty of time to buy clothing once baby has arrived.

Swimsuit

When you start taking your baby swimming or if you go on holiday, you will need a swimsuit. As babies cannot regulate their temperature the way adults can it is important to keep them warm. A wetsuit is a good solution for young babies.

There are different types/designs available and some include Velcro™ or zips to make it easier to get on and off. Often when you buy a swimsuit you will also be able to purchase the matching waterproof hat (which helps keep baby's head out of direct sunlight).

Non-scratch Mittens

It is extremely common for young babies to inadvertently scratch themselves with their nails. Scratch mittens are great to prevent this. The only disadvantage is that the mitten will tend to come off – hence why a lot of sleepsuits have built-in mittens. You can always try using a pair of socks on their hands as an alternative.

Sleeping Bag

A sleeping bag is an alternative solution if you do not wish to swaddle your baby or use tightly tucked blankets. Often a zipped design that allows the baby's arms to be free and prevents their head from being covered when moving. They come in different thicknesses (referred to as togs).

The tog you need is dependent on several factors such as room temperature, baby's age, height and weight. Our 'What to Wear' table will give you some idea of what tog you will require and what the baby will need to wear under it. But always check the latest guidance with the brand you buy from.

Sleeping bags are generally available up to the age of 36 months and usually come in the following sizes:

▶ **0-6 months**
▶ **6-18 months**
▶ **18-36 months**

TEMPERATURE	TOG	WHAT TO WEAR
24–27°C	0.5	or
21–23°C	1	
16–20°C	2.5	or +
12–15°C	3.5	+

Socks/Booties

Socks and baby booties keep your little one's feet nice and warm, especially if you do not have a sleepsuit with integrated feet.

It is not unusual (as with non-scratch mittens) for them to come off and, of course, there is something on the market to solve this problem – an elasticated fabric that pops over socks to keep them secure and to help keep those odd socks at bay!

Pram/Snow Suit

Depending on the season your baby is born in you may or may not need a pram/snow suit straight away. During the colder months the pram suit provides additional warmth, often with a faux fur lining and detachable mitts and feet. Some styles will have integrated foot covers, i.e. non-detachable and typically for younger age brackets.

Foot Warmers/Gloves

If an all-in-one pram suit does not provide detachable mitts and feet or your baby wears a coat, you may want to consider purchasing separate foot warmers (sometimes referred to as fur-lined booties) or gloves to protect their little hands and feet from the elements and keep them warm.

Shoes: Crawler/Pre-walker/Walker

As your child starts to explore and crawl, you may want to protect their little toes when in a public area. 'Pre-walker' or 'Crawler' shoes as they are commonly referred to are lightweight, flexible fitted shoes that make it comfortable for your baby to roam. These shoes are not essential, as it's important in their first year to let them go barefoot, which will help with meeting milestones (feet can breathe and they can feel the floor for stability). However, once they start walking unaided you will want to purchase 'walker' shoes, which have the right support for their feet development.

Sizes come in various widths and half sizes to accommodate rapidly changing feet; feet grow roughly three sizes in a baby's first year and two sizes thereafter until they start school.

GET SET *tip*

CORRECTLY FITTED SHOES ALLOW FEET TO GROW NATURALLY, SO IT IS IMPORTANT TO GET THE RIGHT FIT (MEASURED APPROXIMATELY EVERY 6–8 WEEKS), WHICH YOU CAN HAVE DONE AT YOUR NEAREST CHILDREN'S SHOE SHOP. ALTERNATIVELY, YOU CAN BUY A CHILDREN'S FOOT MEASURE AND MEASURE THEM YOURSELF AT HOME.

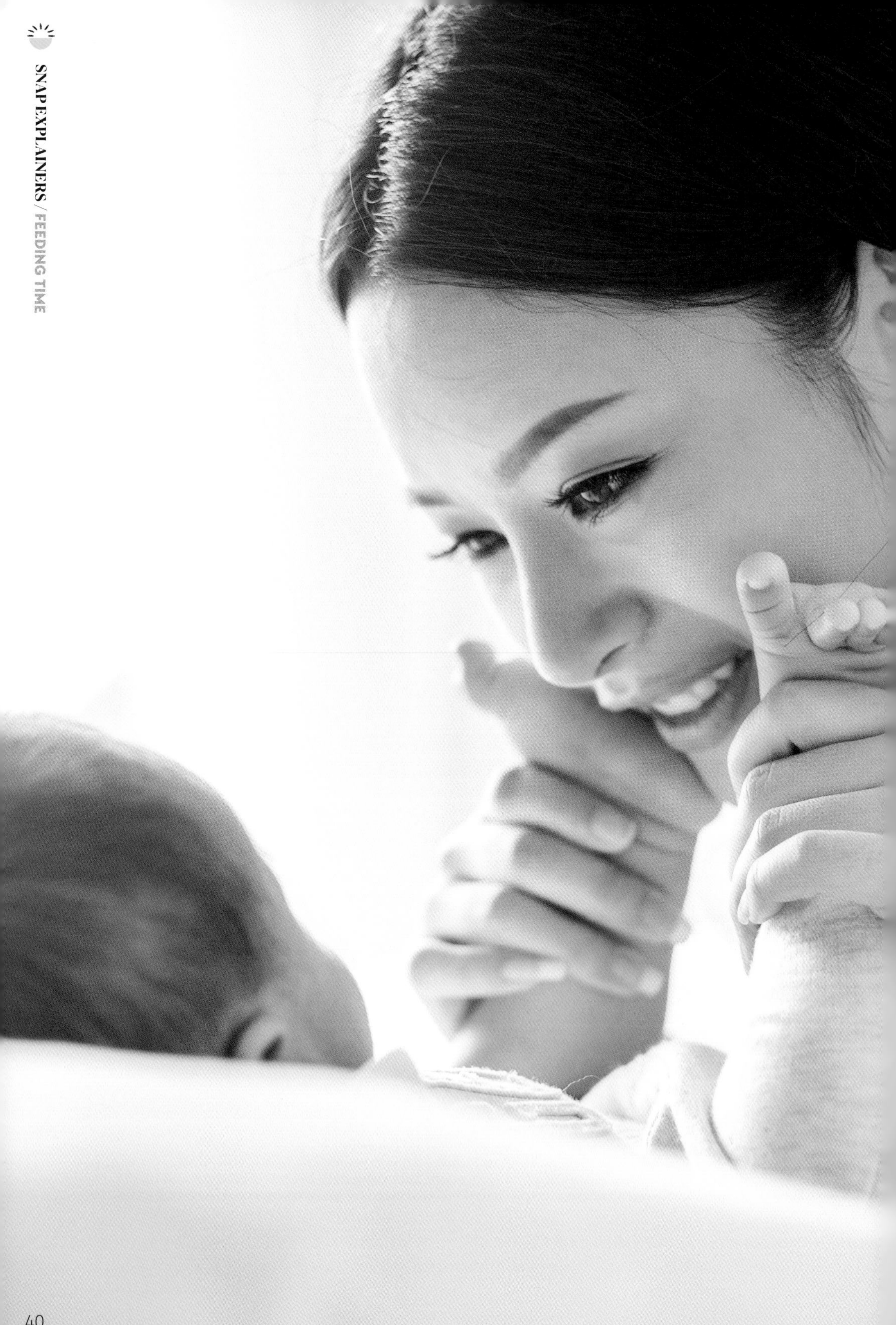

04

FEEDING TIME

ONE OF THE MOST BEAUTIFUL THINGS ABOUT PARENTING IS SEEING THE WORLD YOU
KNEW ALL OVER AGAIN THROUGH ANOTHER SET OF EYES.

Get Set Team

Muslins

These are small cotton cloths used for burping baby and are generally useful to have on hand when needed for clean ups. You will be surprised at just how many you go through in a day! We recommend buying plenty and with lots of lovely colours and designs available, you will not be short on choice.

Dribble Bibs

Dribble, dribble, dribble! As your baby begins to teethe they will dribble a lot and go through multiple bibs throughout the day. A bib will also protect their clothing should they bring up any extra milk, particularly if you have a baby that suffers from reflux (meaning they are susceptible to bringing up milk or are sick during or shortly after feeding – this is quite common and usually gets better by 12 months as the baby's digestive system develops).

Syringe

A syringe helps you to collect your colostrum; a thick and usually golden colour fluid that your breasts produce in the first few days following birth that is full of vitamins and antibodies for baby. Whether you breastfeed or not, colostrum is a very concentrated food that your baby will benefit hugely from in their first few days of life. They only need a small amount at each feed (approximately a teaspoon full).

You can collect and store colostrum in the syringe to make it easier to feed straight to your baby. Your hospital/midwife may give you a syringe but to err on the side of caution we recommend having your own. Many hospitals have dedicated breastfeeding support staff and can help you with this. Antenatal classes also touch on this topic.

Nursing Pillow

As you feed your baby you will want to find a comfortable position. Propping one arm up as baby lays on that side (be it for a bottle or breast feed) will allow your baby to rest comfortably on a pillow that moulds around your body and makes for a more enjoyable feeding experience. An alternative is to test out feeding using a regular pillow at home before deciding if this is something you need.

Tray/Glass Top

This is a separate surface to place baby's feeding equipment on and helps to keep the items clean and disinfected.

Drying Rack/Bottle Tree

A dedicated rack will hold your baby items upright after washing (bottles, teats, brushes, sippy cups, straws etc.), help water drain into the tray below, dry all the water spots and keep your baby bits organised in one place.

Steriliser

Sterilising your baby's feeding equipment is important during their first 12 months whilst their immune system builds. It is also a way to kill any bacteria from formula milk. Items that should be sterilised include bottles, teats, breast pumps, dummies and baby cutlery.

Sterilising products vary and include:

▶ **Microwave steam steriliser** – Add water to the base, place a layer on top, which your bottles sit on, and lock the lid. Pop in the microwave and within a couple of minutes your bottles are sterilised. This offers a portable solution and can be used when travelling (if there is a microwave available). These are typically smaller than electric sterilisers, which means you are limited on the number of items you can sterilise in one go (approximately 4 bottles at a time).

▶ **Electric steam steriliser** – Add water to the heating plate and add your sterilising compartment, which can be one or two modules depending on the product you choose, giving you room to sterilise more items. Pop on the lid and switch on. Your items will be sterilised in about 6 minutes. As a note, the heating plate will need to be descaled (more frequently if you live in an area with hard water). There are specific descaling products available but this can also be achieved using four-parts white vinegar to one-part water.

▶ **Cold water steriliser** – These come in a few sizes for sterilising single or multiple bottles. You simply add a sterilising tablet to the recommended amount of water and your items will be ready within 15 minutes or less.

▶ **The saucepan** – Alternatively, you can submerge bottles (upside down) in a saucepan of boiling water for 5 minutes. Remove and place on a clean surface, drying rack or cloth to allow them to dry.

All methods of sterilisation should keep bottles sterile for 24 hours. However, we would suggest you refer to the manufacturer's guidelines. Additionally, not all bottle sizes/types will fit in all sterilisers, so check this before purchase.

⬛ Dummy/Pacifier/Soother

Dummies, soothers or pacifiers are, as they say on the tin, a tool that can pacify or soothe babies when they are upset or distressed. Whether you choose to offer a dummy or not will come down to personal preference and your baby. If you opt to give your baby a dummy, then you will want a few available since they can get easily lost or dirty when out and about.

In addition to offering comfort to your baby there have been suggestions that a dummy might help prevent Sudden Infant Death Syndrome (SIDS). However, this has not been fully proven and research is ongoing.

For more information on SIDS, read our Minefield Simplifier on page 84.

Dummies are available in various sizes for different age groups. You can also purchase orthodontic dummies (better for teeth development) or even glow-in-the dark ones, saving you time searching for them during the night!

CONSIDERATIONS:

- ▶ **Dependency** – Baby may become dependent on a dummy and unable to settle without one.
- ▶ **Hiding cues** – Crying for hunger, discomfort or wanting attention are cues that can be more difficult to recognise if hidden by dummy use.
- ▶ **Nipple confusion** – If you are breastfeeding and want to use a dummy, it's recommended to only do so once your feeding is established to avoid 'teat' preference and nipple confusion.
- ▶ **Hindering teeth development** – Sucking a dummy or thumb can cause changes to the teeth and jaw such as pushing the upper teeth forward, although it is debated that this is not a problem until the child's adult teeth come through.
- ▶ **Hinder speech development** – Prevents use of sounds to communicate and exploring the full range of tongue movement required to make all speech sounds.

BREASTFEEDING

There is no shortage of breastfeeding information
out there and if this is something you would like to do,
it's worth spending a bit of time focusing on this area
to help you better understand what to expect and how
to best prepare for breastfeeding.

You will not know how you get on with breastfeeding until
your baby arrives, and it's common to find it a challenge
during the first month or so as you establish your supply,
technique and routine. But preparation can help and your
local midwife and antenatal classes are there for this reason
– ask questions and understand the different scenarios
mothers can experience and the actions to deal with these.

In the initial weeks following the birth of your baby,
your healthcare team will also visit you to provide support
and they can advise where your nearest breastfeeding support
clinics/cafés are – this is where you can meet women in similar
situations with professionals on hand to answer
questions and provide support.

La Leche, which is a leading organisation supporting women
worldwide to breastfeed, is a good online resource to learn
more and find local support.

www.laleche.org.uk

For nursing related clothing go to page 78 of our 'Mummy Matters' section.

For breast feeding

● Breast Pads

Breast pads are a thin and absorbent material placed on the inside of your bra and secured using adhesive tape. They absorb any leaking milk which can occur as your body's natural response to baby's feeding time or if your breasts feel engorged, i.e. full. You can buy either disposable or washable pads and change them at regular intervals.

● Nipple Cream

As you establish a feeding technique with your baby and the right 'latch' it is common for mothers to experience sore and cracked nipples. There are creams available to provide relief, commonly known as lanolin, and they may help you to persevere on your breastfeeding journey. Lanolin is non-toxic, fragrance-free and tasteless, and therefore does not require removing before breastfeeding.

Nursing Cover

This is often a large rectangular piece of fabric covering your chest, with a strap that fastens around your neck to hold it in place (known as an 'apron' cover). This can be used for both nursing and expressing, and for when you are out and about or have visitors and want to cover up a little (especially when you are establishing your technique and building confidence). Alternatively, a large muslin/swaddle can also work.

Nipple Shields

A nipple shield is a thin silicone teat that can be placed over a mother's nipple and helps the milk to flow through the holes in the tip and into the baby's mouth. This device can help a baby who is having difficulty learning to breastfeed but it's important to ensure the right position and attachment occurs (as it could result in baby getting less milk) – your healthcare provider will be able to support you with this.

Breast Therapy Gel Pads: Hot & Cold

These mould to the breast and relieve engorgement when used cold or mastitis and blocked milk ducts when used warm. They can also provide general relief.

For Expressed Breast Milk (EBM)

● Expressed Breast Milk Bottles/ Storage Bags

Freezing your milk in specially-designed bags helps retain the nutrients and ensures you have an additional supply available for times when you cannot exclusively breastfeed. Bags are often supplied with a pump, but you may need to purchase them separately if you hire one.

● Breast Pump (for expressing your milk)

A breast pump helps you to express your milk and stimulate your supply so you have more breastmilk to feed your child. This is known as Expressed Breast Milk (EBM).

You can purchase a pump or hire one if you decide that you want to begin expressing. Reasons for expressing can include but are not limited to:

▶ **Increasing milk supply** because your supply seems less than your baby's appetite.
▶ **Relieve engorgement** of the breasts.
▶ **Diagnosed with 'Mammary Hypoplasia'**, which is insufficient glandular tissue developed during adolescence causing low or no milk production. Stimulating your supply might help you to feed or top baby up with your EBM.
▶ **Planning** your feeding schedule.

Depending on how much milk you express, it can be stored in the fridge or freezer and used for top-ups or exclusive feeding via the bottle.

For bottle feeding

● Formula: Instant and/or Powder

Even if you decide you want to breastfeed, it is advisable to purchase a newborn formula 'Starter Kit' to act as a safety net should you need access to formula milk when your baby first arrives.

Scenarios why you may want access to formula milk include your milk not coming in straight away or offering it as a top up to breastmilk. The starter kit typically supplies enough milk for a 24-hour period and comes in ready-made bottles with teats that you screw on top, ready to feed baby.

▶ **Instant milk** – Can be served at room temperature or warmed by placing the bottle directly into a jug containing hot water. Check the temperature at regular intervals until the desired temperature is met. It should not be microwaved as it can produce hot spots. Once instant milk is opened it must be stored in a fridge and consumed within 24 hours or thrown away.

▶ **Powdered milk** – You can prepare powdered milk using a prep machine or a kettle. For this, fill a kettle with at least 1L of fresh tap water (do not use previously boiled tap water), bring to the boil and leave to cool for no more than 30 minutes, so it remains at a temperature of 70°C. Follow the manufacturer's instructions for powder to water ratio.

CONSIDERATION RE 'HUNGRIER BABY' MILK:

▶ When shopping for formula milk you will see brands offer 'hungrier baby' milk, which has people believing it helps baby to sleep for longer as it keeps them fuller for longer. But there is no evidence of this. All milk contains two proteins: casein and whey. It's beneficial to have a higher ratio of whey to casein since casein is harder to digest – only breastmilk has that higher ratio. Hungrier baby milk is supplemented with even more casein, above what is added to regular formula milk. As such, these are not recommended unless advised by your doctor or midwife.

It is also worth noting babies do not always cry because of hunger or continue to suck and take milk for this reason either – it could just be for comfort.

Instant Milk vs Powder

Instant milk is usually available in 200ml or 1L bottles. Alternatively, you can buy powdered milk, which has a longer shelf life and will make up more feeds – this is better value for money, however, instant milk does provide a quick and convenient option.

Moving from Breast to Bottle

It is worth noting that there is no magical solution and you may encounter some struggles when getting your baby to take a bottle after having been breastfed. Our best tip is to persevere, persevere, persevere! Like everything involving a newborn baby, it's a case of trial and error, it does get easier. Use the support network around you!

● Bottles

Bottles come in various sizes (4oz, 6oz, 9oz and 11oz) and styles depending on the brand. There are many bottle brands available advertising different features, so expect to try a few until you discover which type your baby responds well to. Also, your baby will require smaller feeds during the early stages of their life and their requirements in terms of milk will gradually increase as they age. With this in mind, you may want to buy a few of the smaller bottles only in preparation for your baby's arrival and then purchase the larger sizes later, once you know what brand of bottle they have taken to.

Please note: Cows' milk, Soya, Nut and Goats' milks should not be offered to children under 12 months. If your baby has a protein or lactose intolerance then your GP and dietitian will discuss suitable alternatives.

Teats

Teats have different flow rates, i.e. the speed at which the milk comes out, to support your baby's ability to feed more as they grow. When your baby is born they will start on the slowest flow rate and step up from there as they get older.

Brands typically categorise their teat sizes as 1-4, with each size linked to an age range, for example, 1 has the slowest flow rate and is suitable from birth to approximately 2-3 months (brand dependent). Many will also offer an extra slow teat suitable for premature babies. Knowing when to change the teat size will depend on your child's feeding style – if the flow rate seems slower than your baby can tolerate, then you can move up to the next size and vice versa if it seems too fast.

Some of the bottle features available include:

▶ **Anti-colic** – Help to minimise the number of air bubbles in the milk (which can cause upset tummies).
▶ **Teats to imitate the breast** – Particularly appealing to mothers who are mixed feeding (breast & bottle) or moving from exclusively breastfeeding to bottle-feeding, as the teat attempts to provide a more natural feeding experience that resembles the breast.

Bottle Brush

Specially-designed brushes used to help effectively clean your baby's feeding equipment and all of those hard-to-reach areas! You can sterilise this brush along with all of your other baby items.

Please note: Instant milk should not be microwaved as it can produce hot spots.

🌂 Milk Prep Machine

A lot of parents you speak to will tell you that this device was one of their best purchases, and you may well say the same should you choose to go down the bottle-feeding route. They're said to give parents peace of mind for the following reasons:

▶ **Ease of use**
▶ **Prepare milk quickly**
▶ **No fuss preparation**
▶ **Produce the ideal temperature** (which is exactly what you need when preparing for those night feeds!)

A prep machine will make a fresh bottle of milk at just the right serving temperature in less than a few minutes and with just a couple of steps.

🌂 Bottle Warmer

This device helps you to heat milk to the ideal temperature easily and quickly. An alternative method is to place the bottle (filled with formula milk) directly into a jug of boiling water, remembering to check at regular intervals until the desired temperature is met.

Steps to using a milk prep machine:

–1–
Add the required amount of formula powder to your bottle

–2–
Place bottle on the prep machine stand

–3–
Press the button for an initial burst of hot water – once done, shake and dissolve the powder

–4–
Place bottle back on stand and press the button a second time for a longer run of cold water – this will automatically stop once it reaches the required amount

–5–
Give the bottle one last shake, check temperature by pouring a small amount of milk on your wrist, and it's feeding time!

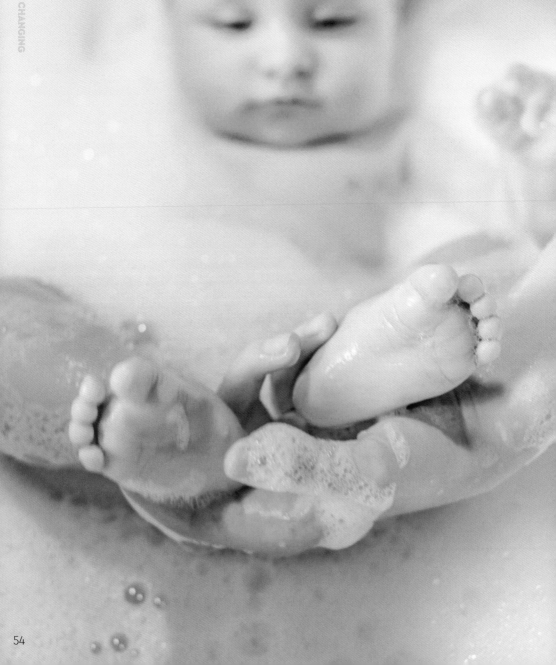

05

SPLASHTIME
& CHANGING

THE BIGGEST SURPRISE, WHICH IS ALSO THE BEST, IS THAT I DIDN'T KNOW
I WOULD LOVE MOTHERHOOD AS MUCH AS I DO.
Deborah Norville

The current guidelines recommend
not bathing your baby until their umbilical
cord stump has fallen off and their belly
button has healed, approximately
1-4 weeks after birth. During this time,
their skin will have formed its natural
protective barrier, so just sponge wash
your child in warm water 2-3 times
a week (or use cotton wool).

Wash Items

Choosing the right products for your child will be a case of trial and error, but there are lots of good brands out there to test. Not all of these items will be required in your baby's first few months but the products you will eventually use are likely to include:

▶ **Bodywash**
▶ **Bubble bath**
▶ **Flannels**
▶ **Hairbursh/comb**
▶ **Sponges**
▶ **Cotton pads**
▶ **Bodycream**
▶ **Shampoo/conditioner**

As early exposure to products can result in allergic reactions or eczema, look for products that are:

▶ **Free of alcohol, colour and perfume**
▶ **Free of parabens and sulphates** – Particularly for haircare products
▶ **Emollient-based** – More suitable for babies with sensitive skin and can soothe dry skin and nappy rash. These are a good option if either parent has a skin condition like eczema

Good to know

TOP AND TAIL
An alternative to full bathing is the 'top and tail' method where you wash your baby's face, neck, hands and bottom using a separate wash bowl of warm water (divided into two sections; one for the top end and one for the tail end).

BABY'S SKIN
This is very sensitive in the first year and it's important to only use products at the right time. For example, you will not need to shampoo or brush your child's hair initially because they won't have much. If you need to clean your baby's head or remove any skin flakes you can use a soft sponge or soft-bristled hairbrush. Additionally, you can find specific haircare products to aid cradle-cap or moisture retention (specifically for children of black and mixed ethnicity).

GET SET *tip*

IF YOU HAVE A BLACK OR MIXED-RACE CHILD, THEN YOU WILL NOT USE A BRUSH BUT A SPECIALIST AFRO COMB OR WIDE-PICK COMB.

Bath Tub

In terms of bathtubs there are several options to choose from:

▶ **Newborn bathtub** – Effectively a bucket-sized unit that you can place anywhere in the house to wash your baby. Some also come with a stand to help ease pressure on your back.

▶ **Bath support** – This sits within your bathtub for your baby to lay on so that they are slightly elevated and easy to reach. Your baby may outgrow this option quite quickly but it's great for providing extra confidence for parents when bathing.

▶ **Growing bathtub** – A larger sized bath that can sit inside the main bathtub or on the floor of the house (while baby does not splash too much). You want one that has an indented mould to comfortably rest your baby's neck and support their spine, as well as a block insert their legs can go around, which prevents them from slipping forward. This also supports them sitting up when they are physically developed enough to do so; a good all-rounder.

▶ **Bath barrier divider** – A bath divider converts a full-sized bathtub into a smaller one (with its rubber edge and suction pads retaining water to one section of the bath). You not only save water, time and energy, but you can reposition the divider to accommodate your baby's growth.

Bath Mat

Placing a non-slip mat inside your bath or shower is highly recommended when you have a newborn. It will reduce the risk of slipping should you decide to have a bath or shower whilst holding your baby. When your baby has outgrown the baby bathtub, you can use the mat for them to sit on inside the main bath.

Nappy Cream

A nappy cream helps prevent soreness and redness from exposure to the acid in urine and faeces. There are plenty of choices on the market to choose from – some will help prevent nappy rash while others will provide treatment should nappy rash occur (which is common).

Nappy sacks

Nappy sacks are always handy to have around and provide a hygienic and convenient way of getting rid of dirty nappies. Use these if you are out and about or not buying a special nappy bin, as they are often scented to disguise odours. Biodegradable options are available.

GET SET *tip*

NAPPY-FREE TIME (ALLOWING BABY
TO KICK ABOUT WITHOUT WEARING
A NAPPY) CAN HELP SOOTHE AND
ELIMINATE NAPPY RASH.

● Nappies

There are various brands offering disposable
and biodegradable nappies and you can even
consider reusable ones. Disposable nappies
come in different sizes based on baby's weight
and an example is provided in the below
table; the plus size is for higher absorbency
and is particularly useful for bedtime (given
that you will want to minimise changes during
the night).

Disposable

NAPPY SIZE	BABY WEIGHT (KG)	BABY WEIGHT (LB)
0	1.5–2.5	3.3–5.5
1	2–5	4.4–11
2	4–8	8.8–17.6
3	6–11	13.3–24.2
4	9–15	19.8–33
4+	10–15	22–33
5	11–17	24–37
5+	12–17	26–37
6	13+ or 15+	28+ or 33+
7	15+	33+

Reusable

NAPPY SIZE	BABY WEIGHT (KG)	BABY WEIGHT (LB)
Newborn	1.8–5.4	4–12
1	3.6–7.2	8–16
2	7.2–15.9	16–35
3	15.9+	35+
BtP Birth to Potty	4.5–5.4	10–12
OSFM One Size Fits Most	up to 13.6	up to 30

There's more and more focus around
using eco-friendly products but what does
it all actually mean?! We cover this
minefield in our 'Nappy Debate' Simplifier
– go to page 88 to read.

Wet Wipes

As with nappies, there are various brands of wet wipes ranging from disposable and biodegradable to sensitive, water-based and head-to-toe options. Finding the right ones that work for your baby's skin will be a case of trial and error at the beginning.

Bath Kneeler

Who is comfortable kneeling on tiles or a hard floor? If you are going to wash your child in the family bath you should consider buying this. A cushioned pad that is placed under your knees constructed from durable water-resistant material. It will offer comfort when kneeling and your knees will thank you for it.

Elbow Rest

Not as much pressure is placed on your elbows as your knees when bathing your baby but it is a tool to keep you comfortable none-the-less while leaning on a hard bathtub.

Bath Thermometer

A thermometer that is placed into the bath water to help you determine if the water temperature is correct. Most designs will flash green if the water temperature is good or flash red if too hot. Even though you may have a good idea of what is the right temperature, a thermometer can introduce a much-needed element of certainty.

Bath Tap Protector

When your baby starts to move around in the bath (between crawling and walking age) you may find they start showing an interest in the tap. This product is a protective cover that is placed over the tap to safeguard babies and small children from potential scalds, bumps and turning the taps on.

Baby Towel

There are specific towels for babies that are smaller in size with some offering an integrated hood, making it quick and easy to wrap your baby up after being removed from the bath. As babies lose most of their body heat through their head, the hood is a useful feature in helping to keep them warm. If you start your baby swimming you may also want to get a hooded swim towel, but in both scenarios you can, of course, use the towels you already have at home.

Bath Toys

Bath time has a practical goal to clean your child, but it can also be fun, which bath toys are great for. This activity can contribute to your child's development such as motor skills and problem solving as they reach for toys, squeeze them and learn what the toys can do. To keep baby engaged and constantly developing their language skills, you can also buy waterproof story books.

Baby Rinse Cup

A cup or jug often with perforated holes which gives you a little more control as you wash shampoo/conditioner out of your child's hair. It also makes for fun play as baby watches you pour water around them.

GET SET *tip*

MOULD CAN BUILD UP INSIDE SQUIRTY TOYS BECAUSE OF WATER RETENTION, SO YOU WILL WANT TO REPLACE THESE TYPES OF TOYS EVERY SO OFTEN OR WHEN YOU SPOT ANY MOULD.

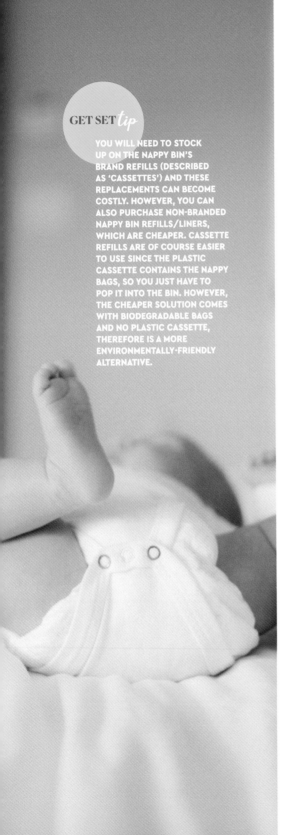

Bath Toy Organiser

There are various choices for organisers, from a set of small drawers to mesh with suction pads that can stick to the bath/bath tiles. These types of solutions will help keep your bathroom tidy and organised.

Nappy Bin & Cassettes

These are specially designed nappy disposal bins and are a quick, tidy and easy way to dispose of dirty nappies. Most importantly, they will help eliminate and lock away unwanted odours!

If using reusable nappies you can buy a nappy bucket to store them in until laundry time. A large wash bag is also a popular alternative, which can be hung on the back of a door and is better when space is at a premium.

Swim Nappies

You will need these if you start taking your baby swimming or are going on holiday and into the pool or sea. They are specially designed nappies that prevent water absorption and have stick-on sides to allow for easy pull on/off. Different sizes are available depending on your baby's weight.

Portable Nappy Caddy

You're about to deal with an urgent nappy change 'poo-explosion alert' only to find the nappies and wet wipes are in another room! Consider investing in a nappy caddy to act as a secondary and mobile nappy change solution, moving from one room to another while keeping those essentials organised in one place.

06

PLAY & DEVELOP

NOTHING BETTER THAN SPENDING AN ENTIRE MORNING STARING INTO MY BABY
DAUGHTER'S EYES, WHISPERING 'I CAN'T DO THIS'.
Ryan Reynolds

Play Mat & Arch

This is a great multi-purpose product for newborns with its soft mat, padded perimeter and toy arch for playtime. It is full of colour, patterns, prints and textured materials to provide stimulation as well as encouraging those key developmental areas (in the early stages).

Large Play Mat

When bubba grows out of the play arch and starts to roll or sit up, jigsaw squares (interlocking foam pieces) or a padded mat (available in different patterns and designs) can provide a soft and safe area for them to play on.

Tummy Roll

After your baby's first few months it is recommended that you allow them some time laying on their front (while being supervised), known as 'tummy time'. The specially designed tummy roll (this looks like a padded circular pillow) helps them develop major motor skills (strengthening their neck and shoulder muscles). It also provides additional stimulation with its colours, patterns and textures.

Tummy time can also be achieved by placing your baby on their stomach while they lay across your legs. Baby might not be too keen when first trying out tummy time but by trying different approaches you should find something that works for you and your baby.

Floor Seat

A supportive seat that helps littles ones get accustomed to sitting up unaided and has a high back for support. They are multi-purpose, offering:

- ▶ **A tray** – Good for weaning and putting toys in front of baby.
- ▶ **A play table** – An additional accessory, which can be easily attached/removed (from the main tray) using suction pads. This provides stimulation and entertainment for baby.
- ▶ **An alternative to the high-chair** – When you enter the weaning/ feeding stage.

Floor seats are typically used between 3–12 months, so even though its use is time-limited, it will aid baby's development once they start being curious about their environment and prefer sitting up to lying down. Refer to the manufacturer's guidelines to check age and weight limits.

Bouncer/Rocker/Baby Swing

Bouncers are a great way to gently rock and soothe baby as well as stimulating them by offering a different position and view of their surroundings. Furthermore, whether you need to rest your arms, take a quick shower, prepare food or put a wash on, place bubba in a bouncer (in the room where you're doing these tasks) and you'll get some much-needed hands-free time to achieve these. There are lots of styles on the market including:

- ▶ **Traditional bouncers** – Use your foot to lightly rock baby back and forth.
- ▶ **Battery-powered bouncers** – Provide a slight bouncing motion and play lullabies.
- ▶ **Swing-style rockers** – Battery operated moving up and down, back and forth or in circles, and plays lullabies – these are typically more expensive.

Your baby may not take to a particular type of bouncer/rocker/swing and as they can be quite expensive, you may want to consider borrowing one or buying this second hand.

Comforter

Often in the form of a small blanket or soft toy, this product is designed to settle babies and, as the name suggests, provide comfort. You may find your baby is drawn to a 'non-designated' comforter such as a muslin, which is perfectly fine (so long as the item is suitable for babies).

GET SET *tip*

IF YOUR BABY IS PARTIAL TO A CERTAIN COMFORTER, CONSIDER BUYING A BACK-UP JUST IN CASE IT SHOULD GET LOST ALONG THE WAY OR DAMAGED BEYOND REPAIR.

Walker/Jumper

You won't need to consider these until your baby starts crawling, cruising, or can hold themselves upright unaided. Baby sits inside a supported seat, which can be adjusted to different height positions, and provides a good source of stimulation and activity with music, lights, rattles and teethers to play with. The key difference between the two is that the walker is on wheels so baby can move around, whereas the bouncer is static with a seat that's suspended and often rotates 360°.

Our resident paediatrician agrees with research suggesting that a walker or jumper used excessively can cause developmental issues in your baby such as:

▶ **Learning incorrect movement patterns** by using their tip toes, which could possibly contribute to a delay in their ability to walk as they spend less time learning to crawl/move around on the floor.
▶ **Losing the opportunity to learn important motor and perceptual skills** such as distance and depth discovered from actively crawling.
▶ **Long-term hip problems** as the hips and knees are taught to take weight in an abnormal position; this is why Canada banned the sale of baby walkers in 2004.
▶ A British medical paper showed that using baby walkers can hinder a child's ability to sit or stand because it holds them upright and **does not allow them to learn the proper balance skills needed for walking**.

If you do decide to purchase a jumper/walker be mindful of the amount of time you allow your baby to use it. This will help avoid/reduce some of the issues highlighted by experts. Alternatively, you may want to consider non-sit walkers that are designed for baby to stand and hold on to for support, which they push along.

Sensory Toys

There are a variety of products available that are great at stimulating your newborn baby and influencing those key development areas. These include:

▶ **Rattles**
▶ **Teethers**
▶ **Items with a musical component**
▶ **Items with a textured touch, patterns and colours**
▶ **Black & white toys** – Newborns can only focus on objects placed between 8-12 inches away from their face and they initially only see black, white and grey (with the distance/colour spectrum becoming greater as the months progress). Therefore, these types of toys are particularly beneficial in the first few months of your baby's life, providing stimulation and entertainment. You might also find your baby is mesmerised by something as simple as your eyes (due to their white and dark appearance).

Teddies

Now who doesn't like a teddy?! If you have teddies saved from your childhood you will love seeing them in your baby's nursery and they will help add to the warmth, personal and loving atmosphere you want to create. Just be sure to check they are age appropriate. If you are gifted any toys/teddies for older ages just put them in a safe place until the time is right.

Books

Start their cognitive development and engage your baby with fairy tales, animated stories or even that novel you have been waiting years to read! Even though baby will not understand the stories right now, just hearing your voice and the different sounds and words will begin the process of language development. Your voice will also bring comfort to your baby and promote the parental bond.

Storage Basket/Cube

When you first have a baby it is amazing how quickly you will start to accumulate toys, blankets and other baby-related items. You may want to invest in a couple of storage solutions such as baskets or cubes. There are lots of designs out there and they come in various materials (such as a woven rope or canvas cotton) to suit all tastes and to complement your home décor.

Baby Milestone Cards/Blanket

This is the perfect way to record your baby's special moments and milestones during their first year such as the date they turn 1 month of age, when they first smile, get their first tooth (and many more). Take a picture that captures baby with their 'milestone' card or blanket, so you can treasure the memories for many years to come!

07

HEALTH & SAFETY

TO BE PREGNANT IS TO BE VITALLY ALIVE, THOROUGHLY WOMAN
AND DISTRESSINGLY INHABITED. SOUL AND SPIRIT ARE STRETCHED – ALONG
WITH BODY – MAKING PREGNANCY A TIME OF TRANSITION, GROWTH
AND PROFOUND BEGINNINGS.
Anne Christian Buchanan

As we work through this chapter we provide guidance on those 'essential' healthcare items to stock at home for your baby. To build your confidence and knowledge in responding to potential accidents and emergencies we would recommend all parents (expectant, new and established) attend a baby first aid course. It is also a good idea to arrange for family members/ grandparents who will be looking after your child to attend a first aid session, not to mention it will be a nice 'preparing for baby' family activity.

🔵 First Aid Kit

It is a good idea to keep a first-aid kit in your house as well as on you whilst out and about. A typical first-aid kit will include items such as:

▶ **Burn shield**
▶ **Plasters**
▶ **Gauze swabs**
▶ **Antiseptic wipes**
▶ **Micropore tape**
▶ **Fabric tape**
▶ **Bandages**
▶ **Safety pins**
▶ **Eye wash**
▶ **Scissors**
▶ **Wound closure strips**

🔵 Thermometer

Aside from the thermometer that might come with your healthcare kit, you may also want to invest in a more advanced model. There are many types available including ones that are placed in the mouth, ear, on the forehead, under the armpit and inside the rectum.

You can use traditional hand-held or digital thermometers, which take readings using a traffic light system. The digital reading is adaptive to the age of your child since 'normal temperatures' vary for different age groups.

🔵 Healthcare/Vanity Kit

These kits come with accessories to help you groom your baby with a few basic healthcare essentials for at home or on the go, such as:

▶ **Nail file**
▶ **Nail clippers**
▶ **Basic thermometer**
▶ **Brush**
▶ **Comb**
▶ **Scissors**
▶ **Nasal aspirator** (this is a nose tube used to help drain any nasal blockages).

Please note: If you opt for a digital ear thermometer, you need to replace the ear cover after each use to prevent cross-infection. Covers are provided with the thermometer but you may need to buy more at a later date.

Baby Toothbrush & Toothpaste

Start brushing your baby's teeth when they first come through. You can begin by simply wiping them with a soft cloth or brushing with a small soft toothbrush and water. Don't worry if you can't brush them much at first, as it is more about getting baby used to the sensation and helping to integrate this process into their daily routine. At a later stage, it is a good idea to add a pea-sized amount of low fluoride toothpaste onto the brush – check the packaging for guidance on ages/ quantities before doing so.

Stair Gate & Locks

Stair gates are highly recommended and should be used from the point your baby starts to crawl. Remember, if you have stairs in your property, then a separate gate should be placed at both the top and bottom of the stairs. Stair gates come in various designs such as retractable, pressure fitted and those that require screwing into the walls. You can purchase gates in different dimensions to fit the space required.

Socket Protectors

By law, all plug sockets must have safety shutters that prevent children from accessing the live terminals. This means that socket covers should not be necessary because even if children put their fingers into plug sockets, they should not be touching any live wires. Having said that, when you start baby-proofing your home (in preparation for your baby crawling and exploring) socket covers will provide an extra level of protection and gives parents peace of mind.

Cupboard Locks

When your baby starts walking (or even just pulling themselves up) they have the freedom to go everywhere and anywhere they want, and they will absolutely love opening and closing (aka banging) cupboard doors! You may therefore want to invest in some cupboard locks. An example is magnet locks, which are secured using an adhesive on the inside door only and a 'magnet key' to open them (therefore maintaining furniture aesthetics).

Corner & Edge Protectors

Safety corner and edge protectors are a childproof solution to protect your baby against injuries from sharp furniture and table corners. This will typically be required once your baby starts cruising (pulling themselves up to standing using aids) and walking.

Foam Door Stoppers

A foam pad that can be placed on the door frame can help prevent those littles fingers from injury and getting accidentally trapped.

Baby Sunscreen

The safest way to protect your baby from harmful sun rays is to keep them well covered and out of direct sunlight. There are suggestions that sunscreen should not be applied to babies until they reach 6 months but recommendations do vary, so always refer to the manufacturer's guidelines before applying to your baby.

Medicine cabinet

● Paracetamol (e.g. Calpol)

Infant paracetamol is available and given orally (via a syringe) making it easier for parents to administer the liquid into baby's mouth.

Often used to alleviate symptoms of:

▶ **Cold**
▶ **Headaches**
▶ **Earache**
▶ **Stomach aches**
▶ **Fever**

CONSIDERATIONS:

▶ Over the counter paracetamol should only be given to children aged 2 months of age, above 4kg in weight, and born after 37 weeks, unless prescribed otherwise by a doctor. The dosage that can be administered is set out by the manufacturer (and is on the packaging).

▶ It is advisable to buy paracetamol in readiness for your baby's first set of injections (around 8 weeks old) and for subsequent injection appointments.

Please note: If you have any doubts then please speak to a professional (pharmacist, midwife, doctor) before administering either Calpol or ibuprofen

● Ibuprofen (e.g. Nurofen)

Infant ibuprofen is available and given orally (again, via syringe).

Often used to alleviate symptoms of:

▶ **Colds**
▶ **Teething/toothache**
▶ **Sprains from injury**
▶ **Fever**

CONSIDERATIONS:

▶ Over the counter ibuprofen should only be given to babies above 3 months of age unless prescribed otherwise by a doctor. The dosage that can be administered is set out by the manufacturer (and is on the packaging).

▶ Ibuprofen is not suitable with certain child illnesses, so check if it is recommended before administering. As an example, ibuprofen cannot be given to children who have chicken pox as it is an anti-inflammatory and will react with the chicken pox, making them go deeper into the skin tissue and potentially causing a more severe secondary condition.

▶ Some children with asthma will not be allowed ibuprofen.

CONSIDERATIONS FOR BOTH:

▶ It can relieve pain but should not be used to alleviate the pain of colic or reflux.

▶ If your child has underlying health issues such as asthma, liver and kidney issues or is small or big for their age, speak to your GP or paediatrician first as dose modification may be required.

▶ There are sugar and colour free options available plus sachets that you can purchase (useful for keeping in the nappy bag when out and about).

● Vitamin D

Breastfed babies should be given a daily vitamin D supplement from birth. Mother's should also take a supplement, which the midwife should cover.

Formula-fed babies who are having more than 500ml of infant formula a day are not required to be given vitamin supplements due to formula milk being fortified with vitamin D and other nutrients.

The NHS recommends all children aged between 6 months to 5 years are given vitamin A, C and D supplements every day because growing children often struggle to get enough of these vital nutrients. You can purchase multivitamin supplements that can be given orally or added to milk/water.

Please note: You should always seek advice from your midwife or GP if you have any uncertainties on which vitamins to give, how and when.

◗ Infacol

A product specifically formulated to relieve wind, infant colic and griping pain. If you believe your baby is suffering from colic then you should speak to your midwife or GP and discuss the options available.

◗ Calamine Lotion

This is a medication used to treat mild skin conditions including sunburn, itching (from minor skin irritations) and heat rash. Typically applied to a cotton wool pad, gently rub over the affected area to relieve symptoms.

Gripe Water

Historically, there has been some negativity surrounding gripe water and in 1992 Britain mandated that alcohol be removed from the product. It is a homeopathic remedy in the form of a liquid supplement (of sodium bicarbonate and herbs) offering natural relief of symptoms such as tummy cramps, spasms and gas. Suitable for babies aged 1 month and above.

Teething Ring or Toy

Teething rings will help soothe your baby's tender gums when needed. They come in solid plastic or filled with a liquid gel, which you can place in the refrigerator to chill. However, the teether should not be frozen as it will become too hard and cold, thus potentially harming your baby's gums.

There are many teething rings and toys available that help soothe gums and provide comfort whilst also offering fun and distraction.

Teething Granules/Gel

These are said to provide symptomatic relief of teething pain and associated symptoms such as flushed cheeks, tender gums and dribbling. You can buy them in the form of:

▶ **Granules** – A homeopathic solution requiring a small amount of the product to be placed on a spoon/palm of hand before giving to the child (using a fingertip).
▶ **Gels** – Most contain a mild anaesthetic and so they need to be bought from a pharmacist. Other options are homeopathic and are available to buy at the supermarket. Apply a small amount directly to the gums or affected area using your fingertip.

CONSIDERATION:

▶ The official NHS advice is to try non-medical soothing methods first like teething rings because there is no strong evidence to suggest that teething gels are effective (and even less in regards to teething granules). What you will find is lots of anecdotal evidence like 'this worked for my baby', and it is true that different strategies can work for different infants. As such, this one will be purely a personal decision and a case of trial and error.

08

MUMMY MATTERS

NO THOUGHT WILL EVER CONSUME MORE SPACE IN YOUR HEART AND MIND
THAN THAT OF YOUR OWN CHILD.

Get Set Team

Maternity Bras

Go to your favourite high street lingerie shop or department store for a maternity and nursing bra fitting. They will advise you on the bras available and ensure they fit you appropriately as your breasts begin to change during your pregnancy. You will typically be fitted for non-underwire bras to allow the breasts to develop freely and aid milk supply production.

It is recommended you check in for a maternity bra fitting every trimester, then two weeks before the baby is due for your nursing bra.

Nursing Bras

These are non-wired bras with cups or straps that unfasten, providing quick and easy access when feeding your baby without having to remove the whole bra! You may find it more comfortable sleeping in your nursing bras, especially when your breasts are full of milk. You will find an array of styles which offer different levels of comfort and support. Your local lingerie shop or department store with a bra-fitting service will measure you for the right sized bra (so you do not need to worry about finding the right ones by yourself).

It's recommended to get fitted two weeks before your due date.

Maternity & Nursing Clothes

- ▶ **Jeans**
- ▶ **Leggings**
- ▶ **Tights**
- ▶ **Dresses**
- ▶ **Tops**

During your pregnancy you may find going up a size or two in dresses and tops will be fine, rather than buying a maternity-specific version. However, many clothes can double up as both a maternity and nursing top/dress. It is worth noting the material and style of the outfit you buy as this has an impact on fit.

For example, a stretch cotton or a-line dress will grow with you during pregnancy and can be used post-pregnancy, giving you better value for your money. But as your bump gets bigger, and depending on the weather, you will want to consider maternity-specific items for your jeans, leggings or tights, as these will accommodate your growing belly and provide all the room you need to be comfortable.

The key feature of nursing tops and dresses is that they often have a double layer around the chest area, and allow you to easily move a small section of the clothing to give your baby quick access to the breast when feeding (used alongside your nursing bra). You will be surprised, once you establish the right technique, at how efficient and discreet breastfeeding can be.

Maternity Support Pillow

As your bump continues to grow and your body changes, you may start to experience some discomfort when lying down in bed. You might find that placing your normal pillow either between your legs or under your hips provides some relief, however, upgrading to a specifically-designed maternity pillow that moulds itself to your body shape can help support your back and bump for a more comfortable night's sleep.

Stretch Mark Cream

Stretch marks are extremely common during pregnancy and occur when your skin stretches rapidly/extensively. They typically appear as parallel lines (with a different texture to your normal skin) and tend to show around the breasts, thighs, bum and tummy.

There are lots of brands available that offer to 'help' but stretch marks are genetic, so do not go crazy on expensive products. It is, however, worth investing in a cream or oil to aid elasticity of the skin and to help the skin feel more nourished.

Maternity Bed Mat

As your expected due date fast approaches, you may want to start placing absorbent mats underneath your bed sheet (and in the car to sit on) just in case your waters break. The mats are usually sealed with a waterproof lining underneath to prevent leakage and the upper layer is made from an absorbent material such as cotton.

Pregnancy Journal

It is amazing how pregnancy flies by and you find yourself forgetting what one month to the next looked like – let alone once bubba arrives! Savouring those special and exciting memories in a journal, not forgetting the physical and hormonal experiences, can be a nice activity to do and will allow you to reflect on your pregnancy journey.

Pregnancy Book

There is an extensive range of pregnancy books available on the market to equip you with the knowledge of what is happening to your body and what to expect as you progress through each trimester. These books can provide guidance, peace of mind and reassurance as you experience lots of different emotions and physical symptoms. You may not manage to finish the book (they are often very detailed) but it will act as a good reference point for the topics you are most interested in pre- and post-pregnancy.

Go to page 117 for your Hospital Bag: What to Pack checklist.

At Hospital and Post-birth

Maternity Pads

In the first few weeks post-birth you will experience what is effectively a heavy period. Regular sanitary towels will not necessarily be suitable and so you may want to consider using these extra thick and ultra-absorbent sanitary pads during this time. Lighter bleeding can still occur for up to 6 weeks after birth, but you should be able to use your regular sanitary towels once you've passed the 'heavy' period.

Peri Bottle/Plastic Jug

You will understandably be a little tender down below post-birth. To help soothe the perineal area (and ease the 'stinging sensation') whilst going to the toilet you should find using a peri bottle or plastic jug to pour water on this area will offer some relief. Using a jug can be challenging but a peri bottle has a thin nozzle spray, which can target the area more effectively by using your hand to squeeze out the water.

Instant Ice or Heat Pack

Instant ice packs have the dual benefit of keeping mum cool during labour and soothing vaginal inflammation post-birth. You just squeeze the bag which breaks the inside and then shake for instant cold application.

An instant heat pack can provide relief to areas such as the lower back and, as with the ice pack, creates heat through squeezing the bag and breaking the contents.

Dual Ice/Heat Pack

There are also non-instant and specific post-partum packs available, which can be used both hot and cold at home. Often filled with a gel, it can be frozen to use cold and then applied to either the perineal area or breasts (to relieve pain and swelling), or to use hot it can be placed in the microwave and then applied to breasts (to relieve engorgement, plugged ducts and mastitis); also known as 'breast therapy gel pads'.

MINEFIELD SIMPLIFIERS

The Complete Guide to Buying for Baby

1.

SIDS

What is Sudden Infant Death Syndrome (SIDS)?

SIDS is the sudden and unexpected death of
a baby where no cause is found in babies under
12 months. For a child over 12 months it is called
Sudden Unexplained Death in Childhood (SUDC).

It was commonly referred to in the past as
'Cot Death' but has been widely abandoned,
since the term was misleading and we now
know SIDS does not only occur if the baby is
asleep in their cot.

THE FACTS

200
The number of lives lost to SIDS in the UK in 2017 – this has reduced by 35% compared to a decade ago.

x6
An infant placed on their front to sleep is 6 times more at risk than one placed on their back.

88%
The percentage of all SIDS deaths that occur in babies who are six months old or less.

82%
SIDS has reduced by 82% since the 'Back to Sleep' message was launched in 1991.

50%
Sharing a room with your baby can halve the risk of SIDS.

1/3
Over 1/3 of SIDS deaths could be avoided if no women smoked during pregnancy.

55%
Just over half of all unexplained infant deaths were boys in 2017.

What causes SIDS?

We do not know what causes SIDS. For many babies it is likely that a combination of factors affects them at a vulnerable stage of their development, which leads them to die suddenly and unexpectedly. Researchers around the world are currently engaged in a number of research projects that aim to find the underlying cause of SIDS and any factors that might suggest that a baby is at higher risk. Whilst it's comparatively rare it can still happen, and there are steps you can take to help reduce the chance of it occurring (particularly important for babies born prematurely or of low birth weight as they are at a higher risk of SIDS).

Safe Sleep Advice to Reduce the Risk of SIDS:

▶ **Place your baby on their back** in a clear cot or moses basket for the first 6 months for all sleeps – day and night.

▶ **Share a room** with your baby for the first six months.

▶ **Keep your baby 'smoke-free'** during pregnancy and after birth – this is one of the most protective things you can do for your baby.

▶ **Never sleep on a sofa or armchair with your baby** as this can increase the risk of SIDS by 50 times.

▶ **Do not co-sleep with your baby** if you or your partner has been drinking, is a smoker, has been taking drugs or is extremely tired; these factors can put babies at an extremely high risk of SIDS when co-sleeping. One study found that the risk of SIDS when co-sleeping is six times higher in smokers than in non-smokers.

Once your baby arrives if you ever worry about the risk of SIDS you can speak with *The Lullaby Trust* support team who can answer your questions on **0808 802 6869** or email info@lullabytrust.org.uk. You can also talk to your midwife or health visitor.

This information has been sourced from The Lullaby Trust, the UK's leading organisation on safe baby sleeping – www.lullabytrust.org.uk.

2.

The nappy debate

To dispose or reuse? That is the question!

Think of a cloth nappy and you might think of a mass of bulky terry cloth secured by a safety pin. If you do, you're certainly not alone, but you're in for a surprise! Cloth nappies have come a long way, and modern versions are becoming more sophisticated with features like increased absorption due to the use of different materials such as bamboo or microfibre. They also comprise of hook and loop fastenings, e.g. Velcro™, poppers or plastic clips, to secure and adjust the fit (to accommodate your growing baby). Sounds pretty good right? The flip side of this is the market is now swamped with hundreds of brands and nappy types. So, what starts as a positive step to helping the environment can quickly become rather overwhelming!

Our aim with this article is to unravel the mass of information to help you ultimately decide; is it worth it?

Let's start with a brief explainer on 'what exactly is a cloth nappy?'

They go by the names:

▶ **Cloth**
▶ **Reusable**
▶ **Washable**
▶ **Real**

They come in 4 styles (because one type just won't do!):

▶ **All-in-one/All-in-two**
▶ **Pocket**
▶ **Fitted/Shaped**
▶ **Pre-fold/Flat**

All styles come with a waterproof shell
– that's the outer nappy layer, which has a waterproof lining (to hold moisture inside) and a microfleece lining that goes against your baby's skin (providing comfort).

Absorbent inserts/liners/boosters are then stuffed inside the nappy to soak up the moisture to keep baby feeling dry.

The key differences between the nappies are:

–1–
Where and how liners are placed (to absorb wee)

–2–
How the nappy is secured

–3–
What liner material is used

Nappy Styles:

All-in-one / All-in-two

Fitted / Shaped

Pocket

Pre-fold / Flat

Images: The Nappy Gurus

	ALL-IN-ONE (AI1) ALL-IN-TWO (AI2)	POCKET	FITTED/SHAPED (TWO-PART)	PRE-FOLD/FLAT/ TERRY SQUARES
WHAT'S IT ABOUT?	**AI1** nappies have inserts that come pre-sewn into the outer shell and are quick to change. **AI2** nappies are similar to AI1 but have an additional liner that can be clipped, snapped or tucked inside the outer shell (to support extra absorbency).	The outer shell has an inside pocket for the absorbent liner to be inserted. These can be assembled in advance.	The 'insert' looks just like a nappy, which you fasten to baby before adding the outer shell. Elasticated at the legs, it provides comfort and flexibility of movement (compared to the terry cloth).	These are similar to the traditional nappy in that they are flat, rectangular cloth diapers folded to fit baby. There is less flexibility at the legs unlike the two-part nappy.
WILL IT ABSORB WETNESS?	More inserts can be added to create extra absorbency as they're often quite slim.	Multiple inserts can be packed into the pocket to find the right absorbency and 'boost'.	Best for highest absorbency and therefore bulkier – ideal choice for bedtime.	Good for absorbency but also bulkier.
HOW DO I FASTEN THE NAPPY?	**Outer shell:** All nappy types have an outer shell that can be secured with a hook and loop fastener or similar, such as Velcro™ and poppers.			
	The length of the nappy can be adjusted using the poppers placed on the front of the outer shell. Good for growing with your child.	Snap the side wings onto the poppers around the waist to secure.	Nappy insert is secured in the same way as the outer shell – with a hook and loop fastener (e.g. Velcro™), poppers, ties or a nippa (a plastic t-shaped grip).	Cloth is typically 'folded' around baby and secured using a nippa. Alternatively, the cloth is folded and placed inside the outer shell (as done for the 'pocket' nappy).
WHEN TO CHANGE (waterproof outer shell and absorbent inserts)	**AI1:** **Both** at every change (requires regular washing so may wear quicker). **AI2:** **Insert** at every change. **Outer shell:** After 2–3 nappy changes (dependent on nappy soiling and wetness).	**Both:** At every change (requires regular washing so may wear quicker).	**Insert:** At every change. **Outer shell:** After 2–3 nappy changes (dependent on nappy soiling and wetness).	**Insert:** At every change. **Outer shell:** After 2–3 nappy changes (dependent on nappy soiling and wetness).

① Materials

Once you decide on your preferred nappy style/s you then have to choose the type of material you want to use on your baby. Different materials have various properties, which determine how effective the nappy can be, e.g. absorption rate, drying speed and how much liquid it can contain. Below is an overview of the different materials available.

PUL (polyurethane laminate) & TPU (thermoplastic polyurethane) – Both are used for the waterproof outer shell on the majority of real nappies with PUL the most commonly used to date. They are both breathable, stretchy, quick to dry, crease-proof, stainproof and, crucially for nappies, waterproof.

Fleece – Light, breathable fabric that picks up moisture and moves it away from the source, spreading it out to be absorbed. This means it's good at creating a feeling of dryness – a great addition to a two-part nappy bedtime routine. It also dries quickly.

Bamboo – Made of finer fibres resulting in a softer, sleeker feel compared to cotton and hemp. It can hold a lot of wetness but is slower to absorb. A great material, particularly for newborns. As it holds onto moisture it takes longer to dry.

Cotton – Is a natural material good at absorbing moisture quickly whilst holding it inside its fibres. But this does mean it takes longer to dry (than synthetic materials). Like fleece, cotton picks up moisture and moves it away from the source, meaning the same area can continue to absorb wetness.

Hemp – Is a natural material (like cotton) but has longer fibres and is therefore is more absorbent. Adding a hemp booster to a nappy, particularly at night, is a simple way to increase the amount that can be absorbed and the speed at which this happens. Hemp can feel rough the more it is used as its fibres are coarser. Even though this makes it durable, it's not as soft and therefore many hemp nappies come with a cotton blend for the right balance.

Microfibre – Is a synthetic fibre and is not recommended to be in contact with skin for long periods of time, which is why these inserts will go inside the waterproof shell pocket. Great at absorbing moisture quickly but can easily leak again. Much like a sponge, if the nappy contains moisture and baby sits on their bum, this could force moisture out – called a 'compression leak'. Microfibre is one of the quicker drying materials.

Did you know?

YOU CAN BUY PRE-LOVED NAPPIES (AKA SECOND-HAND)

And you can make further savings on your initial outlay – although depending on the brand you opt for, the difference between new and pre-owned could be minimal.

SANITISATION

It is important you undertake a thorough wash routine to ensure cloth nappies are clean before using them on your child, eliminating a build-up of wee and dirty stains.

A good wash routine can be followed at www.thenappygurus.com/washing-cloth-nappies

PRINTS

You have an array of fun prints and designs for baby to sport a cute bum look.

SIZE

Many brands offer a size that goes from Birth To Potty (BTP) but some parents find these nappies too large for their baby in the first couple of months, especially if your baby is premature or smaller. Therefore, opt for specific newborn nappies. This will add to your spend but should still be less overall versus the disposable.

Refer to our Nappy Size Guide on page 59.

MORE THAN ONE CHILD?

Using your reusable nappies for subsequent children will result in much larger savings.

ZERO CHEMICALS

Real nappies rely on the material to absorb wetness, unlike disposable nappies, meaning they're bulkier. As such you may need to 'size up' on some of your baby's clothes.

Steps to using a real nappy:

–1–
Choose nappy style

–2–
Attach, fold or stuff the nappy with inserts/linings as needed

TIP: Save time by making up in advance

–3–
Adjust fit on baby for comfort

–4–
Change every 2–3 hours

–5–
Flush any solids down the toilet

TIP: Add a flushable liner to your nappy to make it quicker and easier to dispose of solids

–6–
Place used nappies and washable inserts into a dedicated nappy bucket/large wet bag where you can store them until you're ready to wash them (every 2–3 days to reduce the exposure to ammonia)

GET SET *tip*

THE EASIEST WAY TO DETERMINE EASE OF USE AND PREFERENCE FOR A PARTICULAR STYLE IS TO TEST THEM.

Try before you buy

▶ **Local councils** – Some offer a 'Real Nappy Incentive Voucher Scheme' to promote the use of reusables and to reduce the amount of nappy waste being generated. You can receive a free 'Starter Kit' or cashback once you have purchased your nappies – the amount varies per borough.

Check if your borough offers the scheme by visiting www.thenappygurus.com/councilnappyschemes.

▶ **Nappy libraries** – Are run by volunteers looking to support parents in their quest of moving into reusables and will offer demos.

Visit www.uknappynetwork.org for help on finding your nearest library.

▶ **Real nappy retailers** – Will offer trial packs to purchase and test different nappies before choosing.

Now that's out of the way and you have a better idea of what reusable nappies are, let's get down to business...

② Money matters

Our simple model highlights the average use and spend of **'reusable' vs 'disposable'** nappies during your child's first 2.5 years, based on an average of 7 nappy changes per day. In the first six months you will average closer to 10 nappy changes a day, but this reduces the older they get (approx. 5-8 nappies per day), and dependent on when your child is potty trained (typically starting between 18 months and 2.5 years of age). You can adapt our calculation based on your choice of nappy brands for a more accurate spend.

Disposable vs Reusable

Based on a typical wash cycle of every 3 days, allowing for a few extra to be used during the drying process

	Disposable		Reusable	
	6,388	Total number of nappies	30	
Price ranges across brands: 9-36p	15p	Average cost per nappy	£10	Price ranges across brands: £4-£19
	£958	**TOTAL NAPPY SPEND**	**£300**	
50-60 wipes per pack	1.5 packs	Nappy wipes per week	2 packs	25 cloth wipes per pack
	£1.20	Average cost per pack	£16	
	£234	**TOTAL WIPES SPEND**	**£32**	
	£0	Water & electricity cost	£130	Avg. £1/week
	£1,192	**TOTAL COMBINED NAPPY + WIPE SPEND**	**£462**	

Saving of £730

As demonstrated, reusables provide a sizeable cost saving over the period your child is in nappies.

The initial outlay will be higher for reusables as you buy everything upfront, whereas the cost for disposables, although greater, is spread over this period.

3 **Environment**

This is a hugely important factor for many people nowadays, and consequently the trend and preference for going eco is spilling into the wider consumer market across all industries. So, what are the facts?

THE FACTS

8 million nappies

Disposed of PER DAY in the U.K. alone.

Landfill impact

Disposable nappies are estimated to take around 500 YEARS to decompose and biodegrade.

Global Warming

Most disposable nappies are sold in plastic non-recyclable packaging, which ends up in landfill. The METHANE (produced from landfills and nappy contents as they start to decompose) is hugely damaging and a major contributor to global warming.

Water & Energy

Production of disposable nappies requires 10 TIMES more water and energy than reusables.

Deforestation

The cutting down of trees to provide the wood pulp in the production of disposable nappies is estimated to be in the MILLIONS and affects greenhouse gas emissions, soil erosion, habitats and air pollution.

You will need to use detergent when washing cloth nappies and whilst there are eco-detergents available, they're often not great at tackling soiled nappies. The use of detergent has its own impact on the environment, which needs to be considered. Most modern washing machines are economical with water consumption. In contrast, the waste-water produced from the manufacturing of disposable nappies can be contaminated with chlorine and carcinogens.

It's safe to say that both reusable and disposable nappies have an impact on the environment but research to date suggests that there is a greater negative impact on the environment from using disposables.

④ Time & Space

There is no doubt (or debate) that reusable nappies are more time consuming than disposable ones.

You will need to dispose of the poo, wash, dry and store the nappies, plus it will take extra time putting the nappy together. You should not tumble dry reusable nappies because it will shorten their life span and the waterproof outer shell will degrade over time if exposed to high heat. Air drying is not such an issue during warmer months where they can be hung outside on a clothes line. However, you need to consider those colder months when air drying outside is not an option.

5 Chemicals

Cloth nappies are chemical-free, however, this does not mean babies in cloth are less likely to suffer with nappy rash.

Disposable nappies are thin and absorbent because they contain materials that turn to gel when wet, commonly known as hydrogel. Other chemicals are also used for the dye and patterns as well as the colour change for detecting a wet/soiled nappy. These are chemical reactions taking effect in the nappy whilst baby is wearing it.

MYTH BUSTER

As the chemicals are close to baby's skin, some argue these can cause nappy rash, although this is not proven. Dr Emma Sage, consultant paediatrician, sees rashy bottoms frequently. She explains:

"THE MAIN CAUSE OF NAPPY RASH IS DUE TO A FULLER NAPPY RUBBING AGAINST A BABY'S SKIN RESULTING IN FRICTION AND IRRITATION. THIS WILL HAPPEN REGARDLESS OF THE TYPE OF NAPPY BEING WORN. IT CAN BE MADE WORSE IF BABY HAS AN UPSET STOMACH, IS ON ANTIBIOTICS, HAS PARTICULARLY SENSITIVE SKIN OR A FUNGAL INFECTION."

6 Leakage & Fit

Correctly fitted and 'boosted' reusable nappies, changed at reasonable intervals, should not leak but finding the correct fit and sufficient boosting will take a bit of practice at the beginning.

When your child gets older, they are able to contain their wee for longer, not to mention they drink more. This means you will need to tweak the fit and inserts to accommodate the increased volume in wee. One parent we spoke to explained:

> I USED BAMBOO BOOSTERS AND FOUND THAT THEY WORKED REALLY WELL UP UNTIL MY LITTLE ONE WAS AROUND 18 MONTHS, WHEN IT BEGAN TO LEAK. WE TRIED ADDING EXTRA LAYERS OF COTTON OR HEMP, WHICH HELPED WITH THE ABSORPTION ISSUES.

Some types of real nappies are better at containing breastfed baby poo. Disposable nappies are generally very reliable when it comes to absorbing wetness, but poo explosions are still common. Unlike disposable nappies, real nappies can mask smells. Although this would normally be considered an advantage (particularly when out in public), it can make it more difficult to detect when your baby needs a nappy change.

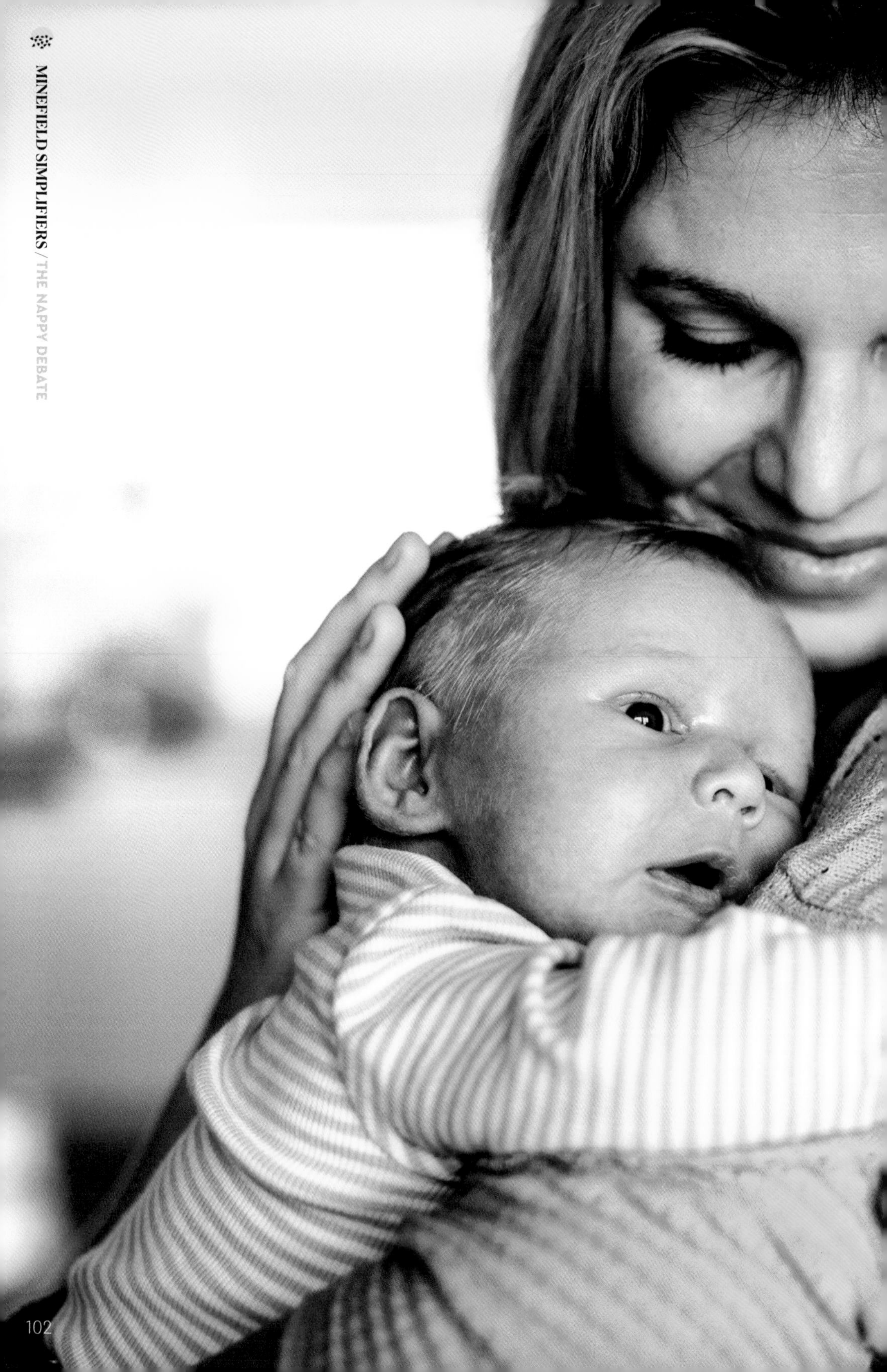

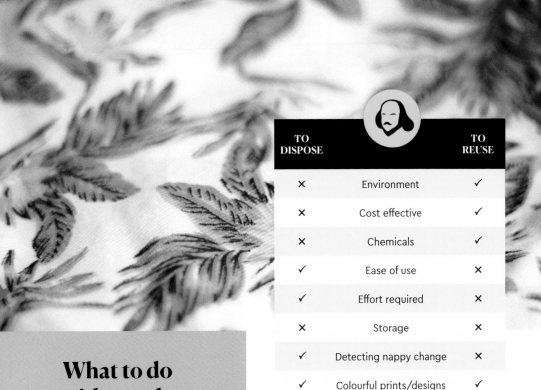

TO DISPOSE		TO REUSE
✗	Environment	✓
✗	Cost effective	✓
✗	Chemicals	✓
✓	Ease of use	✗
✓	Effort required	✗
✗	Storage	✗
✓	Detecting nappy change	✗
✓	Colourful prints/designs	✓

What to do with a real nappy once it's no longer needed?

When the day comes that your little one either no longer fits into their real nappy or no longer needs it, here's what you can do:

REUSABLE
▶ Donate or sell them for the next parent to benefit from.
▶ Keep hold of them if you are planning on having another baby.

NO LONGER REUSABLE
▶ The cloth material can often be recycled – bamboo, for example, is compostable.
▶ The colourful prints can be used for making teddy bears, dolls or cushions.

As you consider whether 'to dispose or not to dispose', we summarise the pros and cons in our Shakespearean table. Ultimately, your decision will be based on whether you feel the cons are a worthy sacrifice in the grand scheme of your parenting journey.

3.

Car Seat Intel

Bringing you up to speed

As we work through this minefield, we will illustrate the types of car seats available, the benefits and considerations for each, and current safety guidelines as approved by the *Royal Society for the Prevention of Accidents* (also known as RoSPA, which is supported by the *UK Department for Transport*). Our aim is to give you a clearer understanding of why you might want a specific type of seat, and to help you to make an informed choice with confidence and speed.

THE LAW

1

Based on current UK Government guidance, children must use a child car seat until they are 12 years old or 135 centimetres tall, whichever comes first. This ultimately means you will buy two or three car seats during this time.

2

There is an exception to the rule for using a car seat, which is when riding in a licensed taxi that does not have a car seat available. When travelling outside of the EU, you should check local country guidance regarding use of car seats.

3

There are two regulatory standards that car seats must meet – ECE **R129** or ECE **R44** (versions /03 or /04) – just look for the orange 'E' label followed by the relevant standard. Both types of seats are approved for use in the UK and EU as long as they are fitted correctly in a vehicle.

R129 is based on height

'i-size' is a new EU safety regulation and runs alongside the older ECE R44 regulation (so parents can choose to buy a seat that meets either R129 or R44.04).

The main changes introduced by R129 are:

▶ **Better protection from side impact** – A 'side-impact crash test' is included as part of the approval process, which the older R44 regulation does not have to pass.
▶ **Easier-to-fit** (attached using ISOFIX).
▶ **Rearward-facing for longer** – Children in this type of seat must remain rear-facing until they are at least 15 months old.

R44 is based on weight

This is the longest standing regulation where car seats have been categorised into specific weight 'groups' (summarised later in this article). It is important to note the last two digits /03 or /04, which indicate approval for legal use. Versions /01 and /02 have not been legal since 2008.

ISOFIX and what you need to know

Car seats can be attached using ISOFIX fittings or seat belts. It is not mandatory to use ISOFIX fittings; however, they were introduced following a large proportion of parents who were unknowingly installing the car seat incorrectly (with a seat belt). All cars made from 2006 should be equipped with ISOFIX anchor points and each car seat manufacturer can advise whether their seat is compatible with your car.

An ISOFIX is a unit that will either come as a separate base to the car seat or integrated into the seat (depending on the model of seat you choose). ISOFIX car seats come with two ISOFIX ports that slot into your car's anchor points. Some come with a support leg, which extends until it rests securely on the floor of the vehicle, between the back and front seats. This is an alternative to the top tether (a fabric strap that attaches the child seat to the tether point often located in the boot of a car), both of which are additional security features of the car seat. The support leg is mainly used for groups 0+ and 1 child seats, both in rear-facing and forward-facing versions.

Car Seat Types

	INFANT CARRIER	CONVERTIBLE OR COMBINATION SEAT	COMBINATION SEAT
WHAT'S IT ABOUT?	**Portable Seat** Allows you to remove it from your vehicle.	**Fixed Seat** Starts off rear-facing until appropriate stage to rotate into forward-facing position.	**Fixed Seat** Converts into a booster at the appropriate stage.
WHO'S IT SUITABLE FOR?	Birth to 87cm Group 0, 0+ (0–13kg) Birth to 15 months	Birth to 105cm Group 0, 0+, 1, 2 (0–25kg) Birth to 7 years	87cm to 150cm Group 1, 2, 3 15 months to 12 years
ORIENTATIONS AVAILABLE	**Rear-facing** A slight recline for baby to lie back in. There may also be the option to lie completely flat once outside the car, for example, when attached to the pram. **Lie-flat** A newer type of infant carrier – there are not many currently on the market. A little more expensive than rear facing because of the extra engineering involved and they can double up as a carrycot (with a compatible pushchair frame).	**Swivel** Often rotating 360°, this will make it easier getting baby in and out of the car. Starting with the car seat facing you (door side), you place baby into the seat and simply rotate them into a rearward– or forward-facing position. **Fixed Seat or 2-Way** A fixed or 2-Way seat starts rearward-facing but will allow a forward-facing position to be configured once your child meets a set height – but no earlier than 15 months if using R129.	**Forward-facing** These are fixed in the forward position and should only be used when it's safe for your child to be transitioned into this position, no sooner than 15 months (but safest at around 4 years). Once the relevant age/height threshold has been reached, this type of seat can be converted into a belt-positioning booster.

107

Our Car Seat Breakdown Guide lends a hand in helping you to determine which category the different types of seats fall within.

Car Seat Breakdown

	HEIGHT 'i-size' ECE R129	WEIGHT ECE RR44/04		APPROXIMATE AGE
INFANT CARRIER Rear-facing or Lie-flat	Birth to 65cm	Birth to 9kg	Group 0	Birth to 6–9 months
	Birth to 87cm	Birth to 13kg	Group 0+	Birth to 12–15 months
COMBINATION Swivel or 2-Way	45cm to 105cm	Birth to 18kg	Group 0, 0+, 1	Birth to 4 years
	61cm to 105cm	Birth to 25kg	Group 0+, 1, 2	Birth to 7 years
	65cm to 105cm	9kg to 18kg	Group 1	Approx. 6–9 months to 4 years
FORWARD-FACING	87cm to 150cm	9kg to 36kg	Group 1, 2, 3	15 months to 12 years
	105cm to 150cm	15kg to 36kg	Group 2, 3	Approx. 4 to 12 years

Each car seat 'type' will offer plenty of choice accommodating different heights and weights. As such, many seats are classified as a multi-group – one which spans more than one group, will accommodate your child's growth, and will last for a longer period of time.

SECURING YOUR CHILD IN THE SEAT

5 point harness

The majority of seats will come with a 5-point-harness 'seatbelt', which distributes the force of an impact across 5 points – two at the shoulders, two at the hips, and one where the harness buckles between the legs.

Impact shield

Alternatively, you will come across some seats that provide an impact shield, which spreads the force of a collision across the entire seat and protects sensitive body areas.

Both of these are additional safety features protecting your child in case of an accident. Once your child reaches a minimum weight of 15kg, the car's 3-point seatbelt can then be used to secure your child.

Benefits and Considerations

INFANT CARRIER

BENEFITS:

- ✓ **Portable** – Allowing you to carry baby in the car seat for those quick errands or moving from car to house.
- ✓ **Minimal disturbance to baby** –When asleep (moving from one place to another).
- ✓ **Attaches to pram system** – Saves you taking the carrycot (or needing a carrycot if you purchase a lie flat).
- ✓ **Good for parents without a car** – To use in taxis or for car hire (with or without the ISOFIX base).
- ✓ **Lie-flat** – Allowing your baby to lie flat in the car encourages healthy development of your baby's spine, and a greater recline allows babies to inhale optimally. It is common that babies who sit in upright car seats for a period of time often slump a little, which can restrict their breathing.
- ✓ **Lie-flat** – Good alternative for very low birth weight babies.

CONSIDERATIONS:

- ▶ **Maximum weight will be reached within 6–15 months** depending on the seat you buy.
- ▶ **ISOFIX base has to be purchased separately** from the carrier – so do not get caught out with the car seat retail price, add the ISOFIX base price for a total cost (if you opt for an ISOFIX).
- ▶ **Check which 'next stage' car seats are compatible with the ISOFIX base**, so when the time comes to transition your child you know what the choices are. You cannot use other brands' seats on your ISOFIX, so if you opt for another brand you will need to buy another base (if you have an ISOFIX).
- ▶ Although carriers are used for transporting baby (be it in a car, pram, or from one building to another), **you still need to take them out after two hours** for safety reasons.

CONVERTIBLE/COMBINATION SEAT

BENEFITS:

✓ **Will last longer than the infant carrier** since they are designed to grow with your baby (up to around 4 or 7 years).

✓ Ability to transport baby in the **rearward-facing position for longer** (up to 4 years).

✓ **Converts to a forward-facing position** (when baby reaches the appropriate height/weight).

✓ **Swivel function** will save you awkward physical contortions and an aching back by putting your child into the vehicle door-entry side.

✓ **Cost effective**, as you will only require two car seats from birth up until 12 years of age:
  - COMBINATION SEAT: swivel/fixed or groups 0–1/2, followed by;
  - FORWARD-FACING SEAT or groups 2/3. It is not uncommon for parents to buy three car seats if they opt for an infant carrier first.

CONSIDERATIONS:

▶ **Not portable** like the infant carrier.

▶ **Less convenient** for carrying out quick errands/short trips – setting up the pram can be more time consuming than just picking up the carrier.

▶ **Greater chance of disturbance** when baby is asleep carrying them out of the car to the pram/house, particularly in the winter months when you will need to put them in their pram suit/coat.

▶ To keep your child rearward-facing after using an infant carrier (which is recommended) you can buy either:
  - MULTI-GROUP CAR SEAT covering groups 0, 0+, 1 (birth up to 4 years).
  - MULTI-GROUP CAR SEAT covering groups 0+, 1, 2 (up to 7 years).
  - i-size 129 SEAT suitable for carrying a child up to 105cm.

FORWARD-FACING

BENEFITS:

✓ **Final car seat** up to 12 years.

✓ Moving straight to this category from an infant carrier means **you will not need to purchase another car seat**.

CONSIDERATIONS:

▶ If you purchase an infant carrier, **you will find yourself looking for the next stage car seat from ages 9–15 months** (depending on the seat you buy). Some forward-facing-only seats are available from 9kg or 67cm, which is around 9 months old. But, if for example your child is 9kg (or more) and below the legal age to face forward (15 months), then it will be too early to buy this type of seat. In this case, consider a seat from groups 0+, 1, 2.

▶ **A forward-facing seat is safest** once your child reaches the maximum height or weight limit in groups 1 (around 4 years) or 2 (around 7 years).

?

Did you know?

You cannot put your child in a car seat with padded clothing such as a jacket or pram suit, because the harness is then not secured properly to your child. Pull the harness for a snug fit against your child's body – the straps should be just tight enough that you can slip two fingers flat between your child's body and their collar bone.

AND REMEMBER!

REARWARD-FACING

Current safety guidelines recommend keeping your baby rearward-facing for as long as possible (up to approximately 4 years), with the minimum age until they can face forward being 15 months. This is because a rear-facing seat spreads the force of a crash more evenly across the back of the car seat and child's body.

The manufacturer of your specific car seat will have guidance on when your child can face forward, for example, a 0–4 year old swivel seat (R129 'i-size') allows you to keep your child rearward-facing up to 105cm (around 4 years). But you are permitted to face them forward from 76cm (upwards of 15 months).

AGE GUIDANCE

All brands will give you an indication of the age your child should remain in the seat, but take these as guidelines only because the deciding criteria will be either your child's height or weight.

Consequently, you may find your child will need to move to the next stage car seat earlier than the age indicator (taller/heavier) or later (smaller/lighter). In some cases, this can vary as much as 6 to 12 months.

CAR COMPATIBILITY

Not all car seats are compatible with all car models, therefore the supplier should conduct a car safety check for you at the point of purchase. Alternatively, you can check the manufacturer's guidelines or website to understand the seat's compatibility with your car.

SECOND-HAND? NO!

It is not recommended to purchase car seats second hand because you will not know its history, such as whether the seat has been in an accident or not. Also, general wear and tear may render the seat unsafe, and its date of production may mean it does not conform to current safety standards. This is one corner you don't want to cut.

2-HOUR RULE!

Do not allow your baby to be in the car seat for longer than 2 hours. Take them out for a break, even if it means waking them up. On unavoidable long journeys it is recommended to break for 15–30 minutes every two hours. Therefore, be sure to allow for the extra journey time.

LEAVING HOSPITAL

Should you have your baby in a hospital, you will need a car seat to take them home in as you cannot be discharged without one. However, this is not applicable for home births or if travelling back via public transport.

NEWBORN INSERT

All newborn/group 0, 0+ car seats should come with a newborn insert to provide extra security and compactness for baby in their first months.

CHANGE

Irrespective of the seat you have, always change it when the maximum weight or height thresholds are reached.

Review the Government's latest car seat governance and safety standards online at www.gov.uk/child-car-seats-the-rules.

Visit www.rospa.com to learn more from The Royal Society for the Prevention of Accidents.

GET SET TOOLS

The Complete Guide to Buying for Baby

GET SET *tip*

SAVE ON SPACE BY BUYING
TRAVEL-SIZED TOILETRIES
OR DECANT THE ONES
YOU ALREADY HAVE INTO
SMALLER CONTAINERS.

HOSPITAL BAG
What to pack

As your due date fast approaches preparation is key, and so we would recommend getting your hospital bag packed between two to four weeks before baby is due.

You should make sure that you pack enough to cover a couple of nights in hospital including both practical and home comfort essentials. This will help you to feel as relaxed as possible. We cover all this in our Hospital Bag: What to Pack checklist, and if for any reason you have to stay in hospital for a little longer, your partner/family can always pick up additional things for you from home.

What to Pack will include items for mum-to-be, baby and birthing partner. You can pack everything altogether or alternatively take a separate bag for each. It is, however, worth remembering that there is likely to be limited space around the hospital bed, so try to focus on the important items and your bag size when packing.

Our list is comprehensive and, outside of the essential items, what you decide to pack will be dependent on whether the hospital will supply these items, what you want your ideal labour environment to be, and personal choices. We have therefore tagged these items as non-essential versus essential.

Mum

ESSENTIALS

- **Birth plan**
- **Hospital notes**
- **Purse**
- **Phone & charger**
- **Snacks/drinks**
  – e.g. nuts/energy bar, chocolates/sweets, bottled soft drinks/water

CLOTHING

- **Labour outfit**
  i.e. loose-fitting clothes
- **Pyjamas/nightie/open front shirt** (good for breastfeeding and skin-to-skin contact)
- **Knickers x6** disposable or dark coloured underwear you don't mind throwing away (high-waisted if you are having a caesarean)
- **Clothes for coming home in** e.g. loose dress
- **Shoes** e.g. slip-on shoes are particularly useful if you are having a caesarean
- **Flip-flops** for walking around and getting in the shower
- **Nursing bra x1**
- **Dressing gown**
- **Disposable/cheap slippers**
- **Socks x3**
- **Glasses/contact lenses** (if applicable)

LABOUR ENVIRONMENT

- **Eye mask** to help relax and sleep (shutting out hospital ward lights)
- **Ear plugs** to reduce noise if staying in hospital
- **Headphones** for music
- **Speaker** for music in the delivery unit
- **Handheld fan**
- **Book/Kindle/tablet**
- **Room spray**
- **Pillow** from home
- **Photos** e.g. baby scan /family pic
- **Instant heat packs**
- **Instant ice packs**
- **TENS machine** (if applicable – check hospital availability with midwife)
- **Exercise ball** (if applicable – check hospital availability with midwife)

POST-BIRTH

- **Maternity pads x1 pack**
- **Breast pads**
- **Peri bottle/plastic jug**
- **Nipple cream**

TOILETRY BAG

- **Any personal medicine**
- **Deodorant**
- **Toothbrush & toothpaste**
- **Shower gel/soap**
- **Shampoo/conditioner**
- **Hairbursh & hairbands /clips**
- **Lipbalm**
- **Mouthwash**
- **Antibacterial gel/wipes**
- **Hand cream**
- **Facial moisturiser/ toner/wipes/cotton pads**
- **Body lotion**
- **Flannel**
- **Make-up** if you plan on having some photos taken in the hospital with your new family

Baby

CLOTHING
- Sleepsuit x3
- Bodysuit x3
- Baby hat x2
- Mitts x2 pairs
- Socks/booties x1
- Cardigan x1 particularly when transporting baby home
- Blankets x2
- Coming home outfit x1
- Vest bodysuit x2 add as an extra layer underneath a bodysuit in case baby or environment is particularly cold
- Swaddle
- Jacket/pramsuit if taking baby home in the pram

CHANGING
- Nappies x10 & nappy sacks place the nappy inside the sack so you don't need to fiddle around in hospital
- Wet wipes
- Nappy cream
- Cotton wool
- Baby sponge
- Dummies (if using)

FEEDING
- Formula milk starter kit
- Muslins x4
- Feeding bottles x2 small (if applicable – check hospital availability with midwife)
- Syringes to collect your colostrum (if applicable – check hospital availability with midwife)

Birthing partner

ESSENTIALS
- Birth plan (both have a copy)
- Phone & charger/battery pack charger
- Money for car park/download car park app
- Snacks/drinks e.g. nuts/energy bar, chocolates/ sweets, bottled soft drinks/water

CLOTHING
- Underwear x3
- Socks x3
- Change of clothes
- Empty carrier bags in case you want to separate dirty washing/clean clothes
- Swim outfit to help mum in the shower or birthing pool if desired

PRE-BIRTH
- Book/magazines
- Glasses/contact lenses (if applicable)
- Headphones

TOILETRY BAG
- Any personal medicine
- Deodorant
- Toothbrush & toothpaste
- Comb/brush
- Moisturiser

GOING HOME
- Car seat for car or taxi
- Pram for bus or train

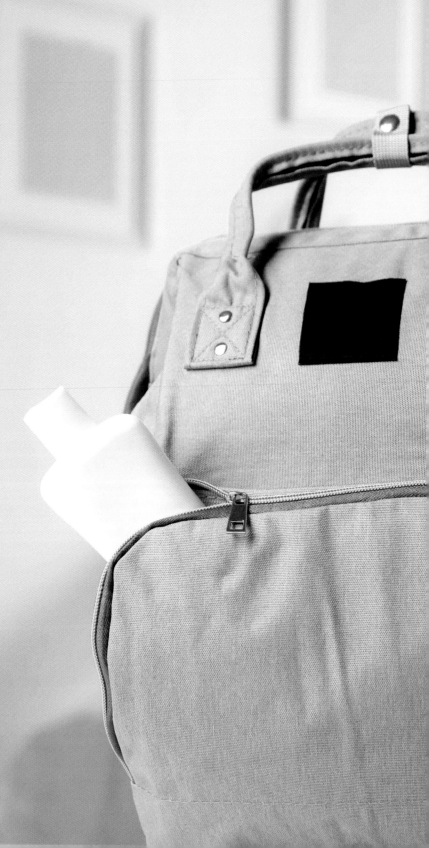

NAPPY BAG
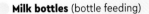
Must-haves

- **Milk bottles** (bottle feeding)
- **Milk** (instant/powder/EBM)
- **Nursing cover/large muslin** (if breastfeeding)
- **Thermos flask**
- **Wet wipes**
- **Nappies**
- **Nappy sacks**
- **Nappy cream**
- **Travel changing mat**
- **Muslin**
- **Dribble bibs**
- **Dummy/pacifier**
- **Dummy steriliser**
- **Toys/comforter/books**
- **First aid kit**
- **Nipple cream**
- **Antibacterial wipes/gel**
- **Sunscreen**
- **Pack of tissues**
- **Change of clothes** (including bodysuit, replacement outfit, hat, mittens and socks)
- **Blanket**
- **Purse/phone/keys**
- **Snacks for mum**
- **Spare top for mum**

The ultimate
CHECKLIST

LITTLE ONE'S ROOM

- Bedside crib & mattress
- Moses basket & mattress
- Cot & mattress
- Mattress sheets x2
- Waterproof mattress cover x1 per sleep station
- Changing mat x1-2
- Blankets x2-3
- Baby monitor
- Room thermometer
- Baby monitor holder
- Sleeping pod/nest
- Swaddles x2
- Wardrobe
- Chest of drawers
- Changing table
- Nursing chair/rocking chair
- Lambskin comforter
- Blackout blinds/curtains
- White noise machine
- Cot/crib bumpers
- Cot mobile
- Projector night light
- Bookshelves
- Framed pictures
- Wall art
- Spiral toy - cot

OUT & ABOUT

- Pram: carrycot & pushchair
- Car seat
- Baby-on-board sign
- Nappy bag/rucksack
- Weekend/travel bag
- Stroller/buggy
- Pram liner/footmuff
- Pram organiser
- Cupholder
- Rearward-facing mirror
- Car window shades
- Travel cot/sleeping pod
- Nappy pouch
- Baby carrier/sling
- Sun parasol/shade for pram/stroller
- Beach parasol
- Formula pots x4-6
- Thermos flask
- Dummy steriliser
- Lanyards x1 pack (approx. 6 in a pack)
- Travel steriliser
- Travel play mat

BABYWEAR

- Bodysuit x10 (mix of short and long)
- Sleepsuit/baby grow x8
- Romper x2-4
- Jackets/cardigans x2-3
- Beanie/woolly hat x2
- Sun hat x2
- Outfits x2-4
- Swimsuit
- Non-scratch mittens x4
- Sleeping bag x2
- Socks/booties x6
- Pram/snow suit x1
- Foot warmers/gloves x1
- Shoes: crawler/pre-walker & walker

FEEDING TIME

- ○ Muslins x8–10
- ○ Dribble bibs x6–10
- ○ Syringe
- ○ Steriliser
- ○ Nursing pillow
- ○ Tray/glass top
- ○ Drying rack/bottle tree
- ○ Dummy/pacifier x4

For Breastfeeding

- ○ Breast/nursing pads
- ○ Nipple cream
- ○ Nursing cover x1
- ○ Nipple shields
- ○ Breast therapy gel pads
  – hot & cold

For Expressed Breastmilk (EBM)

- ○ Breast pump
- ○ Expressed breastmilk bottles/storage bags

For Bottle Feeding

- ○ Formula: instant and /or powder
- ○ Bottles & teats: 4oz-6oz x4 9oz-11oz x4
- ○ Bottle brush
- ○ Milk prep machine
- ○ Bottle warmer

SPLASHTIME & CHANGING

- ○ Bath tub
- ○ Bath mat
- ○ Nappy cream
- ○ Nappy sacks
- ○ Nappies
- ○ Wet wipes
- ○ Bath kneeler
- ○ Elbow rest
- ○ Bath thermometer
- ○ Bath tap protector
- ○ Baby towel x2–3
- ○ Bath toys
- ○ Baby rinse cup
- ○ Bath toy organiser
- ○ Nappy bin & cassettes/ nappy bucket/large wet bag
- ○ Swim nappies
- ○ Portable nappy caddy

Baby Wash Items

- ○ Bodywash
- ○ Bubble bath
- ○ Flannels
- ○ Hairbrush/comb
- ○ Sponges
- ○ Cotton pads
- ○ Bodycream
- ○ Shampoo/conditioner

PLAY & DEVELOP

- ○ Play mat & arch
- ○ Large play mat
- ○ Tummy roll
- ○ Floor seat
- ○ Bouncer/rocker/baby swing
- ○ Comforter x1–2 (back-up)
- ○ Sensory toys
- ○ Walker
- ○ Jumper
- ○ Teddies
- ○ Books
- ○ Storage basket/cube
- ○ Baby milestone cards/ blanket

HEALTH & SAFETY

- First aid kit
- Healthcare/vanity kit
- Thermometer
- Baby toothbrush & toothpaste
- Stair gate & locks
- Socket protectors
- Cupboard locks
- Corner & edge protectors
- Foam door stoppers
- Baby sunscreen

Medicine Cabinet

- Paracetamol
- Ibuprofen
- Vitamin D
- Infacol
- Calamine lotion
- Gripe water
- Teething ring or toy
- Teething granules/gel

MUMMY MATTERS

- Maternity support pillow
- Stretch mark cream
- Maternity bed mat
- Pregnancy journal
- Pregnancy book

Maternity/Nursing Clothes

- Maternity bras x4
- Nursing bras x4
- Jeans x1-2
- Leggings x1-2
- Tights x1-2
- Dresses x1-2
- Tops x2

At Hospital and Post-birth

- Maternity pads
- Peri bottle/plastic jug
- Instant ice pack
- Instant heat pack
- Dual ice/heat pack

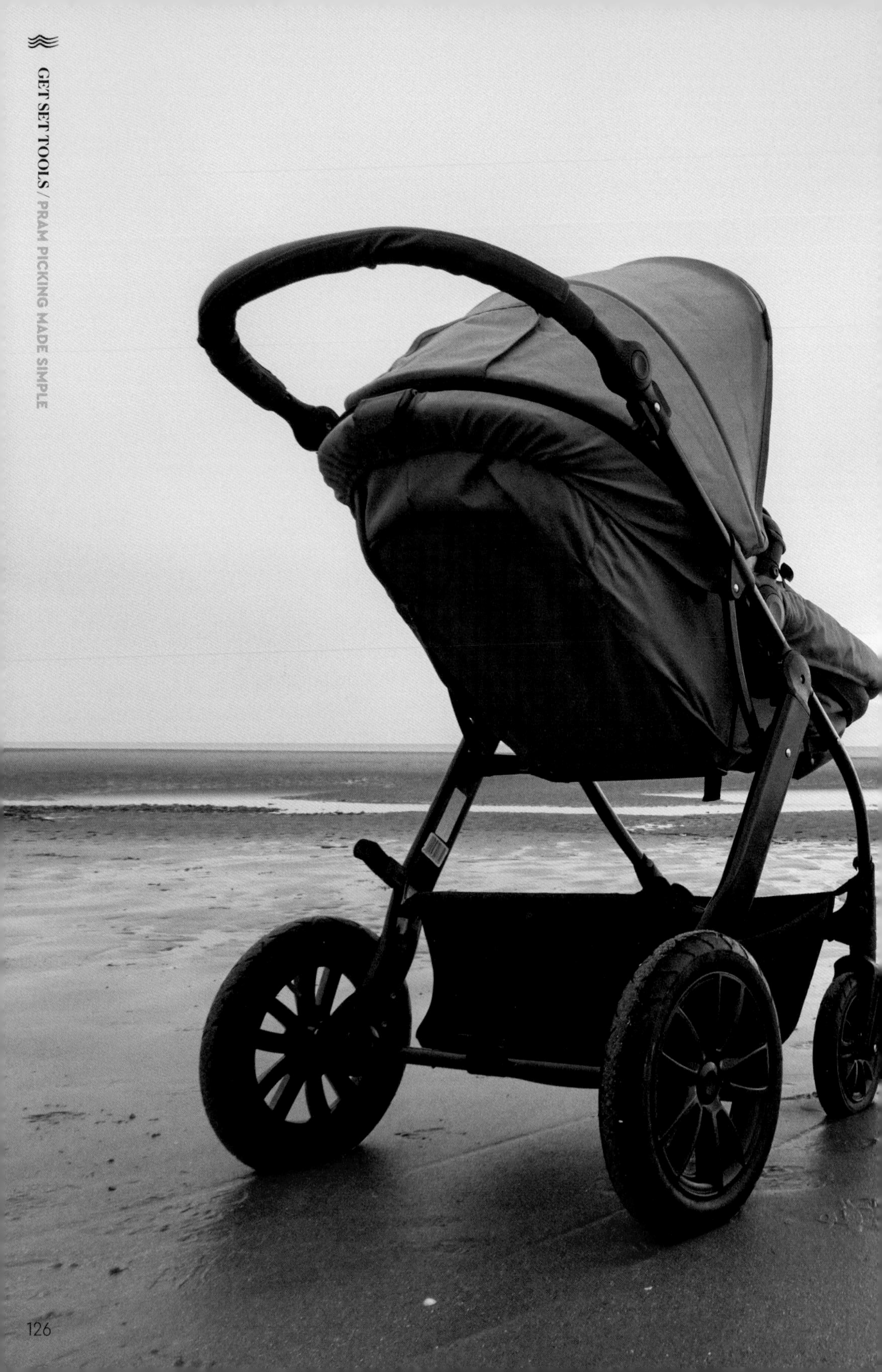

PRAM PICKING
Made simple

Use this template to compare different prams as you research online or visit stores.

Some features may not be a priority when picking a pram, but having a clear snapshot of these and their benefits will allow you to make a decision with confidence. Some accessories have to be purchased separately (with the exception of the rain cover, pram basket and travel adapters, which often come as part of the bundle). Don't be afraid to ask if additional accessories can be included within the package – the sales attendant will want to seal the deal!

Fill in as you go....

BRAND & PRODUCT

FEATURES

Dual seat system (able to carry x2 children)

Carrycot suitable for overnight sleeping

Pushchair – 'lay-flat' recline position

Rearward & forward-facing pushchair

Car seat compatibility

Integrated sun canopy (UV 50+)

Suitable for uneven terrain, e.g. appropriate wheels

Pram basket – good size

EASE OF USE

Easy to manoeuvre/steer

Easy to collapse

Adjustable handlebar (with different height settings)

SIZE

Weight

Can easily store at home

Can easily fit in boot of car

DESIGN

Colours/print

Material

COMFORT & SAFETY

Seat belt fastens securely and easily

Brakes easy to put on/off

Pram feels sturdy

Supplied with a bumper bar

ACCESSORIES

Raincover included

Carrycot stand (for indoors)

Pram organiser

Cup holder

Travel adapters included (to attach car seat to base)

Matching nappy bag

Sun parasol

Pram liner

Footmuff

PRICE

GET SET *tips*

• ASK IF THE RETAILER WILL LET YOU TRY THE SEAT FIRST
  BEFORE BUYING AS YOU WILL FEEL MORE COMFORTABLE
  ONCE YOU HAVE TESTED COMPATIBILITY

• CHECK WHAT THE RETURN POLICY IS

• IF YOU OPT FOR AN INFANT CARRIER YOU MAY WANT
  TO NEGOTIATE A DISCOUNT FOR BUYING BOTH YOUR
  'NEWBORN' AND 'NEXT STAGE' CAR SEATS AT THE
  SAME TIME (SO LONG AS BUDGET PERMITS). IF YOU
  PURCHASE A SEAT THAT GOES FROM BIRTH TO 4 YEARS,
  YOU WILL NOT NEED TO WORRY ABOUT THE NEXT STAGE
  CAR SEAT FOR SEVERAL YEARS

• ASK ABOUT CAR SEAT ACCESSORIES AND IF ANY CAN
  BE INCLUDED AS PART OF THE PRICE, OR DISCOUNTED.
  THESE CAN INCLUDE ADAPTERS, A RAINCOVER AND
  SUNSHIELD. IF YOU DON'T ASK, YOU DON'T GET!

CAR SEAT
Selector

Find your ideal car seat with ease using our template and tips. Whether you go into a retailer or shop online, there should be trained staff who are knowledgeable in talking through the features of their car seats and can show you how to install it, or provide support such as videos.

Fill in as you go....

PRODUCT NAME				
SEAT TYPE				
Height/weight allowance				
Age guidance				
Accessories included (what?)				
Compatible with my car?				
Compatible with my pushchair?				

Colour choices

Price of car seat

ISOFIX base required?

Price of ISOFIX base?

What next stage car seats are
compatible with base?

Price of next stage car seat?

TOTAL PRICE

My notes

My notes

My notes

My notes

My notes

My notes

GET SET MUM

My notes

My notes

Thank you so much for taking the time to read this guide.